AWS Encryption SDK Developer Guide

A catalogue record for this book is available from the Hong Kong Public Libraries.

Published in Hong Kong by Samurai Media Limited.

Email: info@samuraimedia.org

ISBN 9789888407828

Contents

What Is the AWS Encryption SDK?   6
Where to find more information 6

How the AWS Encryption SDK Works   8
Symmetric Key Encryption 8
Envelope Encryption 8
AWS Encryption SDK Encryption Workflows 9
    How the SDK Encrypts Data 10
    How the SDK Decrypts an Encrypted Message 10

Concepts in the AWS Encryption SDK   11
Data Keys 11
Master key 11
Master key operations: Generate, Encrypt, Decrypt 12
Master key provider 12
Cryptographic Materials Manager 12
Algorithm Suite 13
Encryption Context 13
Encrypted Message 13

Getting Started with the AWS Encryption SDK   15

Supported Algorithm Suites in the AWS Encryption SDK   16
Recommended: AES-GCM with Key Derivation and Signing 16
Other Supported Algorithm Suites 16

AWS Encryption SDK Programming Languages   18

AWS Encryption SDK for Java   19
Prerequisites 19
Installation 19

AWS Encryption SDK for Java Example Code   20
Encrypting and Decrypting Strings 20
Encrypting and Decrypting Byte Streams 22
Encrypting and Decrypting Byte Streams with Multiple Master Key Providers 24

AWS Encryption SDK for Python   28
Prerequisites 28
Installation 28

AWS Encryption SDK for Python Example Code   29
Encrypting and Decrypting Strings 29
Encrypting and Decrypting Byte Streams 30
Encrypting and Decrypting Byte Streams with Multiple Master Key Providers 32

AWS Encryption SDK Command Line Interface   36

Installing the AWS Encryption SDK Command Line Interface   37
Installing the Prerequisites 37
Installing the AWS Encryption CLI 37

How to Use the AWS Encryption SDK Command Line Interface   39

How to Encrypt and Decrypt Data 39
How to Specify a Master Key 39
    Master Key Parameter Attributes 40
    How to Specify Multiple Master Keys 41
How to Provide Input 41
How to Specify the Output Location 42
How to Use an Encryption Context 42
How to Store Parameters in a Configuration File 44

Examples of the AWS Encryption SDK Command Line Interface   **46**
Encrypting a File 46
Decrypting a File 48
Encrypting All Files in a Directory 49
Decrypting All Files in a Directory 51
Encrypting and Decrypting on the Command Line 52
Using Multiple Master Keys 54
Encrypting and Decrypting in Scripts 56
Using Data Key Caching 58

AWS Encryption SDK CLI Syntax and Parameter Reference   **62**
AWS Encryption CLI Syntax 62
AWS Encryption CLI Command Line Parameters 63
Advanced Parameters 65

Data Key Caching   **66**

How to Implement Data Key Caching   **67**
Implement Data Key Caching: Step-by-Step 67
Data Key Caching Example: Encrypt a String 69

Setting Cache Security Thresholds   **73**

Data Key Caching Details   **74**
How Data Key Caching Works 74
    Encrypt Data without Caching 74
    Encrypt Data with Caching 75
Creating a Cryptographic Materials Cache 76
Creating a Caching Cryptographic Materials Manager 77
What Is in a Data Key Cache Entry? 77
Encryption Context: How to Select Cache Entries 78

Data Key Caching Example   **79**
LocalCryptoMaterialsCache Results 79

Data Key Caching Example in Java   **81**
Producer 81
Consumer 83

Data Key Caching Example in Python   **86**
Producer 86
Consumer 87

LocalCryptoMaterialsCache Example AWS CloudFormation Template   **90**

Frequently Asked Questions   **95**

AWS Encryption SDK Reference   **97**

AWS Encryption SDK Message Format Reference   **98**

Header Structure 98

Body Structure 100

     Non-Framed Data 100

     Framed Data 101

Footer Structure 102

Body Additional Authenticated Data (AAD) Reference for the AWS Encryption SDK   **103**

AWS Encryption SDK Message Format Examples   **104**

Non-Framed Data 104

Framed Data 107

AWS Encryption SDK Algorithms Reference   **110**

AWS Encryption SDK Initialization Vector Reference   **112**

Document History for the AWS Encryption SDK Developer Guide   **113**

What Is the AWS Encryption SDK?

The AWS Encryption SDK is an encryption library that helps make it easier for you to implement encryption best practices in your application. It enables you to focus on the core functionality of your application, rather than on how to best encrypt and decrypt your data.

The AWS Encryption SDK answers questions like the following for you:

- Which encryption algorithm should I use?
- How, or in which mode, should I use that algorithm?
- How do I generate the encryption key?
- How do I protect the encryption key, and where should I store it?
- How can I make my encrypted data portable?
- How do I ensure that the intended recipient can read my encrypted data?
- How can I ensure my encrypted data is not modified between the time it is written and when it is read?

Without the AWS Encryption SDK, you might spend more effort on building an encryption solution than on the core functionality of your application. The AWS Encryption SDK answers these questions by providing the following things.

A Default Implementation that Adheres to Cryptography Best Practices
By default, the AWS Encryption SDK generates a unique data key for each data object that it encrypts. This follows the cryptography best practice of using unique data keys for each encryption operation.
The AWS Encryption SDK encrypts your data using a secure, authenticated, symmetric key algorithm. For more information, see Supported Algorithm Suites in the AWS Encryption SDK.

A Framework for Protecting Data Keys with Master Keys
The AWS Encryption SDK protects the data keys that encrypt your data by encrypting them under one or more master keys. By providing a framework to encrypt data keys with more than one master key, the AWS Encryption SDK helps make your encrypted data portable.
For example, you can encrypt data under multiple AWS Key Management Service (AWS KMS) customer master keys (CMKs), each in a different AWS Region. Then you can copy the encrypted data to any of the regions and use the CMK in that region to decrypt it. You can also encrypt data under a CMK in AWS KMS and a master key in an on-premises HSM, enabling you to later decrypt the data even if one of the options is unavailable.

A Formatted Message that Stores Encrypted Data Keys with the Encrypted Data
The AWS Encryption SDK stores the encrypted data and encrypted data key together in an encrypted message that uses a defined data format. This means you don't need to keep track of or protect the data keys that encrypt your data because the AWS Encryption SDK does it for you.

With the AWS Encryption SDK, you define a master key provider that returns one or more master keys. Then you encrypt and decrypt your data using straightforward methods provided by the AWS Encryption SDK. The AWS Encryption SDK does the rest.

Where to find more information

If you're looking for more information about the AWS Encryption SDK and client-side encryption, try these sources.

- To get started quickly, see Getting Started.
- For information about how this SDK works, see How the SDK Works.
- For help with the terms and concepts used in this SDK, see Concepts in the AWS Encryption SDK.
- For detailed technical information, see the AWS Encryption SDK Reference.
- For help with questions about using the AWS Encryption SDK, read and post on the AWS Key Management Service (KMS) Discussion Forum that the AWS Encryption SDK shares with KMS.

For information about implementations of the AWS Encryption SDK in different programming languages.

- **Java**: See AWS Encryption SDK for Java, the AWS Encryption SDK Javadocs, and the aws-encryption-sdk-java repository on GitHub.
- **Python**: See AWS Encryption SDK for Python, the AWS Encryption SDK Python documentation, and the aws-encryption-sdk-python repository on GitHub.
- **Command Line Interface**: See AWS Encryption SDK Command Line Interface, Read the Docs for the AWS Encryption CLI, and the aws-encryption-sdk-cli repository on GitHub.

If you have questions or comments about this guide, let us know! Use the feedback links in the lower right corner of this page.

The AWS Encryption SDK is provided for free under the Apache license.

How the AWS Encryption SDK Works

The AWS Encryption SDK uses *envelope encryption* to protect your data and the corresponding data keys. For more information, see the following topics.

Topics

- Symmetric Key Encryption
- Envelope Encryption
- AWS Encryption SDK Encryption Workflows

Symmetric Key Encryption

To encrypt data, the AWS Encryption SDK provides raw data, known as *plaintext data*, and a data key to an encryption algorithm. The encryption algorithm uses those inputs to encrypt the data. Then, the AWS Encryption SDK returns an encrypted message that includes the encrypted data and an encrypted copy of the data key.

To decrypt the encrypted message, the AWS Encryption SDK provides the encrypted message to a decryption algorithm that uses those inputs to return the plaintext data.

Because the same data key is used to encrypt and decrypt the data, the operations are known as *symmetric key encryption and decryption*. The following figure shows symmetric key encryption and decryption in the AWS Encryption SDK.

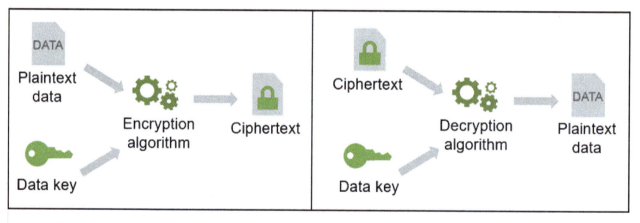

Envelope Encryption

The security of your encrypted data depends on protecting the data key that can decrypt it. One accepted best practice for protecting the data key is to encrypt it. To do this, you need another encryption key, known as a master key. This practice of using a master key to encrypt data keys is known as *envelope encryption*. Some of the benefits of envelope encryption include the following.

Protecting Data Keys
When you encrypt a data key, you don't have to worry about where to store it because the data key is inherently protected by encryption. You can safely store the encrypted data key with the encrypted data. The AWS Encryption SDK does this for you. It saves the encrypted data and the encrypted data key together in an encrypted message.

Encrypting the Same Data Under Multiple Master Keys

Encryption operations can be time-consuming, particularly when the data being encrypted are large objects. Instead of reencrypting raw data multiple times with different keys, you can reencrypt only the data keys that protect the raw data.

Combining the Strengths of Multiple Algorithms

In general, symmetric key encryption algorithms are faster and produce smaller ciphertexts than assymetric or *public key encryption*. But, public key algorithms provide inherent separation of roles and easier key management. You might want to combine the strengths of each. For example, you might encrypt raw data with symmetric key encryption, and then encrypt the data key with public key encryption.

The AWS Encryption SDK uses envelope encryption. It encrypts your data with a data key. Then, it encrypts the data key with a master key. The AWS Encryption SDK returns the encrypted data and the encrypted data keys in a single encrypted message, as shown in the following diagram.

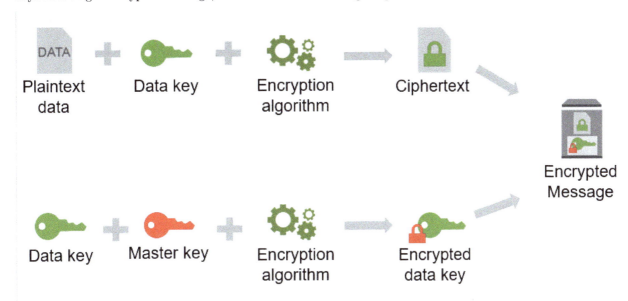

If you have multiple master keys, each of them can encrypt the plaintext data key. Then, the AWS Encryption SDK returns an encrypted message that contains the encrypted data and the collection of encrypted data keys. Any one of the master keys can decrypt one of the encrypted data keys, which can then decrypt the data.

When you use envelope encryption, you must protect your master keys from unauthorized access. You can do this in one of the following ways:

- Use a web service designed for this purpose, such as AWS Key Management Service (AWS KMS).
- Use a hardware security module (HSM) such as those offered by AWS CloudHSM.
- Use your existing key management tools.

If you don't have a key management system, we recommend AWS KMS. The AWS Encryption SDK integrates with AWS KMS to help you protect and use your master keys. You can also use the AWS Encryption SDK with other master key providers, including custom ones that you define. Even if you don't use AWS, you can still use this AWS Encryption SDK.

AWS Encryption SDK Encryption Workflows

The workflows in this section explain how the SDK encrypts data and decrypts encrypted messages. They show how the SDK uses the components that you create, including the cryptographic materials manager (CMM), master key provider, and master key, to respond to encryption and decryption requests from your application.

How the SDK Encrypts Data

The SDK provides methods that encrypt strings, byte arrays, and byte streams. For code examples showing calls to encrypt and decrypt strings and byte streams in each supported programming languages, see the examples in the Programming Languages section.

1. Your application passes plaintext data to one of the encryption methods.

   To indicate the source of the data keys that you want to use to encrypt your data, your request specifies a cryptographic materials manager (CMM) or a master key provider. (If you specify a master key provider, the AWS Encryption SDK creates a default CMM that interacts with your chosen master key provider.)

2. The encryption method asks the CMM for data keys (and related cryptographic material).

3. The CMM gets a master key from its master key provider. **Note**
   If you are using AWS Key Management Service (AWS KMS), the KMS master key object that is returned identifies the CMK, but the actual CMK never leaves the AWS KMS service.

4. The CMM asks the master key to generate a data key. The master key returns two copies of the data key, one in plaintext and one encrypted under the master key.

5. The CMM returns the plaintext and encrypted data keys to the encryption method.

6. The encryption method uses the plaintext data key to encrypt the data, and then discards the plaintext data key.

7. The encryption method returns an encrypted message that contains the encrypted data and the encrypted data key.

How the SDK Decrypts an Encrypted Message

The SDK provides methods that decrypt an encrypted message and return plaintext strings, byte arrays, or byte streams. For code examples in each supported programming languages, see the examples in the Programming Languages section.

1. Your application passes an encrypted message to a decryption method.

   To indicate the source of the data keys that were used to encrypt your data, your request specifies a cryptographic materials manager (CMM) or a master key provider. (If you specify a master key provider, the AWS Encryption SDK creates a default CMM that interacts with the specified master key provider.)

2. The decryption method extracts the encrypted data key from the encrypted message. Then, it asks the cryptographic materials manager (CMM) for a data key to decrypt the encrypted data key.

3. The CMM asks its master key provider for a master key that can decrypt the encrypted data key.

4. The CMM uses the master key to decrypt the encrypted data key. Then, it returns the plaintext data key to the decryption method.

5. The decryption method uses the plaintext data key to decrypt the data, then discards the plaintext data key.

6. The decryption method returns the plaintext data.

Concepts in the AWS Encryption SDK

This section introduces the concepts used in the AWS Encryption SDK. The AWS Encryption SDK is designed so that you can use the default implementations of the components without detailed knowledge about their functionality. This section is provided as a glossary and reference.

Topics

- Data Keys
- Master key
- Master key operations: Generate, Encrypt, Decrypt
- Master key provider
- Cryptographic Materials Manager
- Algorithm Suite
- Encryption Context
- Encrypted Message

Data Keys

A *data key* consists of cryptographic material. It is the secret key that protects the data that you encrypt.

Data keys are generated by master keys. You do not need to implement or extend data keys to use the AWS Encryption SDK. When a master key generates a data key, it returns two copies of the data key; one in plaintext and one that is encrypted by the master key that generated it. The plaintext data key can be encrypted by multiple master keys, each of which returns an encrypted copy of the data key. Every encrypted data key is associated with the master key that encrypted it and the master key provider that supplied the master key.

When you encrypt data in the AWS Encryption SDK, the encrypted data keys are stored in an encrypted message along with the encrypted data.

In the AWS Encryption SDK, we distinguish *data keys* from *data encryption keys*. Several of the supported algorithm suites, including the default suite, use a key derivation function that prevents the data key from hitting its cryptographic limits. The key derivation function takes the data key as input and returns a data encryption key that is actually used to encrypt the data. For this reason, we often say that data is encrypted "under" a data key rather than "by" the data key.

Master key

A *master key* encrypts, decrypts, and generates data keys.

The AWS Encryption SDK represents master keys as abstract classes or interfaces so you can implement the master key operations in the way that best meets the security requirements of your organization. For example, although they are called "keys," master keys might not have their own cryptographic material. Also, unlike data keys, whose use and algorithm suite are strictly defined by AWS Encryption SDK, master keys can use any algorithm suite or implementation.

Master keys are instrumental to envelope encryption. In envelope encryption, one master key generates and encrypts a data key that is used to encrypt data. Other master keys then re-encrypt the plaintext data key. As a result, any master key is sufficient to decrypt the data.

Each master key is associated with one master key provider that returns one or more master keys to the caller.

The AWS Encryption SDK provides several commonly used master keys, such as AWS Key Management Service (AWS KMS) customer master keys (CMKs), raw AES-GCM (Advanced Encryption Standard / Galois Counter Mode) keys, and RSA keys. You can implement your own master keys for other cryptographic algorithms and services. For example, you could implement master keys backed by implementations of Elliptical Curve Integrated

Encryption Scheme (ECIES), Key Management Interoperability Program (KMIP), tokenization services, or other proprietary systems.

Master key operations: Generate, Encrypt, Decrypt

Master keys in the AWS Encryption SDK generate, encrypt, and decrypt data keys. You write methods to perform these operations when you create a master key, but your application does not call the methods directly. The SDK calls them when you ask it to encrypt or decrypt data.

You can implement the master key methods in the way that works best for your organization. For example, when asked to generate a data key, a master key can create or return a key in any way that fulfills the requirements of the algorithm suite that they use. Master keys can generate data keys locally or remotely. They can derive the keys algorithmically, call a service that generates the cryptographic material, or return previously-generated data keys. The SDK requires only that they return a valid data key object.

Also, although master keys must implement all three methods, you can create master keys that actually perform only one or two of the three operations. Calls to the remaining methods just fail or return errors. These limited master keys might be useful in a system with strict access controls that do not let the same users encrypt and decrypt data.

All master key operations take an encryption context as input. For optimal security, master key operations that encrypt data keys should cryptographically bind the encryption context to the encrypted data so that changing any key or value in the encryption context invalidates the encryption. Master key operations that decrypt should verify the encryption context and fail unless they include the same encryption context used to encrypt. The encryption context is most useful when there are users who have permission to decrypt, but not encrypt.

Master key provider

A *master key provider* returns objects that represent master keys. Each master key is associated with one master key provider, but a master key provider typically provides multiple master keys.

The simplest master key provider always returns the same master key. In fact, master keys are implemented as master keys providers that only return themselves. More complex master key providers might use key rotation, the encryption context, application permissions, and other factors to select master keys from among the set they can provide.

Many master keys providers wrap or extend other master key providers to customize their behavior and functionality. For example, a custom master key provider might select a master key provider from a collection, delegate requests, and combine their results.

Cryptographic Materials Manager

The cryptographic materials manager (CMM) gets the cryptographic materials that are used to encrypt and decrypt data. The *cryptographic materials* include plaintext and encrypted data keys, and an optional message signing key. You can use the Default CMM that the AWS Encryption SDK provides (`DefaultCryptoMaterialsManager`) or write a custom CMM.

Each Default CMM is associated with a master key provider. When it gets a materials request, the Default CMM gets master keys from its master key provider and uses them to generate the requested cryptographic material. This might involve a call to a cryptographic service, such as AWS Key Management Service (AWS KMS).

In each call to encrypt or decrypt data, you specify a CMM or a master key provider. This lets you choose a particular set of master keys for the operation. You can create a CMM explicitly and specify its master key provider, but that is not required. If you specify a master key provider in an encryption request, the SDK creates a Default CMM for the master key provider.

Because the CMM acts as a liaison between the SDK and a master key provider, it is an ideal point for customization and extension, such as support for policy enforcement and caching.

Algorithm Suite

The AWS Encryption SDK supports several algorithm suites, all of which use Advanced Encryption Standard (AES) as the primary algorithm, and combine it with other algorithm and values.

The AWS Encryption SDK establishes a recommended algorithm suite as the default for all encryption operations. The default might change as standards and best practices improve. You can specify an alternate algorithm suite in requests to encrypt data or when creating a cryptographic materials manager (CMM), but unless an alternate is required for your situation, it is best to use the default. The current default is AES-GCM with an HMAC-based extract-and-expand key derivation function (HKDF), Elliptic Curve Digital Signature Algorithm (ECDSA) signing, and a 256-bit encryption key.

If you specify an algorithm suite, we recommend an algorithm suite that uses a key derivation function and a message signing algorithm. Algorithm suites that have neither feature are supported only for backward compatibility.

Encryption Context

To improve the security of your cryptographic operations, use an encryption context in all requests to encrypt data. The encryption context is optional, but recommended.

An *encryption context* is a set of key–value pairs that contain arbitrary nonsecret data. The encryption context can contain any data you choose, but it typically consists of data that is useful in logging and tracking, such as data about the file type, purpose, or ownership.

In requests to encrypt data, you can include an encryption context along with the plaintext data and a master key provider. The AWS Encryption SDK cryptographically binds the encryption context to the encrypted data so that the same encryption context is required to decrypt the data. The AWS Encryption SDK also includes the encryption context in the encrypted message that it returns, along with the encrypted data and data keys. The encryption context in the encrypted message always includes the encryption context that you specified in the encryption request, along with elements that the operation might add, such as a public signing key.

To decrypt the data, you pass in the encrypted message. Because the AWS Encryption SDK can extract the encryption context from the message, you do not need to pass it in separately. After decrypting the data, the AWS Encryption SDK returns a result that includes that encryption context along with the plaintext data. The functions in your application that decrypt data should always verify that the encryption context in the decrypt result includes the values that you expect before it returns the plaintext data.

When choosing an encryption context, remember that it is not a secret. The encryption context is displayed in plaintext in the header of the encrypted message that the SDK returns. If you are using AWS Key Management Service, the encryption context also might appear in plaintext in audit records and logs, such as AWS CloudTrail.

Encrypted Message

Encrypt operations in the AWS Encryption SDK return an encrypted message and decrypt operations take an encrypted message as input. An *encrypted message*, a formatted data structure that includes the encrypted data along with encrypted copies of the data keys, the algorithm ID, and, optionally, an encryption context and a message signature.

Combining the encrypted data and its encrypted data keys streamlines the decryption operation and frees you from having to store and manage encrypted data keys independently of the data that they encrypt.

For technical information about the encrypted message, see Encrypted Message Format.

Getting Started with the AWS Encryption SDK

To use the AWS Encryption SDK, you need a master key provider. If you don't have one, we recommend using AWS Key Management Service (AWS KMS). Many of the code samples in the AWS Encryption SDK require an AWS KMS customer master key (CMK).

To interact with AWS KMS, you need to use the AWS SDK for your preferred programming language, such as the AWS SDK for Java or the AWS SDK for Python (Boto). The AWS Encryption SDK client library works with the AWS SDKs to support master keys stored in AWS KMS.

To prepare to use the AWS Encryption SDK with AWS KMS

1. Create an AWS account. To learn how, see How do I create and activate a new Amazon Web Services account? in the AWS Knowledge Center.

2. Create a customer master key (CMK) in AWS KMS. To learn how, see Creating Keys in the *AWS Key Management Service Developer Guide*. **Tip**
   To use the CMK programmatically, you will need the ID or Amazon Resource Name (ARN) of the CMK. For help finding the ID or ARN of a CMK, see Viewing Keys in the *AWS Key Management Service Developer Guide*.

3. Create an IAM user with an access key. To learn how, see Creating IAM Users in the *IAM User Guide*. When you create the user, for **Access type**, choose **Programmatic access**. After you create the user, choose **Download.csv** to save the AWS access key that represents your user credentials. Store the file in a secure location.

   We recommend that you use AWS Identity and Access Management (IAM) access keys instead of AWS (root) account access keys. IAM lets you securely control access to AWS services and resources in your AWS account. For detailed best practice guidance, see Best Practices for Managing AWS Access Keys

   The `Download.csv` file contains an AWS access key ID and a secret access key that represents the AWS credentials of the user that you created. When you write code without using an AWS SDK, you use your access key to sign your requests to AWS. The signature assures AWS that the request came from you unchanged. However, when you use an AWS SDK, such as the AWS SDK for Java, the SDK signs all requests to AWS for you.

4. Set your AWS credentials using the instructions for Java or Python and the AWS access key in the `Download.csv` file that you downloaded in Step 3.

   This procedure allows AWS SDKs to sign requests to AWS for you. Code samples in the AWS Encryption SDK that interact with AWS KMS assume that you have completed this step.

5. Download and install the AWS Encryption SDK. To learn how, see the installation instructions for the programming language that you want to use.

Supported Algorithm Suites in the AWS Encryption SDK

An *algorithm suite* is a collection of cryptographic algorithms and related values. Cryptographic systems use the algorithm implemenation to generate the ciphertext message.

The AWS Encryption SDK algorithm suite uses the Advanced Encryption Standard (AES) algorithm in Galois/Counter Mode (GCM), known as AES-GCM, to encrypt raw data. The SDK supports 256-bit, 192-bit, and 128-bit encryption keys. The length of the initialization vector (IV) is always 12 bytes; the length of the authentication tag is always 16 bytes.

The SDK implements AES-GCM in one of three ways. By default, the SDK uses AES-GCM with an HMAC-based extract-and-expand key derivation function (HKDF), signing, and a 256-bit encryption key.

Recommended: AES-GCM with Key Derivation and Signing

In the recommended algorithm suite, the SDK uses the data encryption key as an input to the HMAC-based extract-and-expand key derivation function (HKDF) to derive the AES-GCM encryption key. The SDK also adds an Elliptic Curve Digital Signature Algorithm (ECDSA) signature. By default, the SDK uses this algorithm suite with a 256-bit encryption key.

The HKDF helps you avoid accidental reuse of a data encryption key.

This algorithm suite uses ECDSA and a message signing algorithm (SHA-384 or SHA-256). ECDSA is used by default, even when it is not specified by the policy for the underlying master key. Message signing verifies the identity of the message sender and adds message authenticity to the envelope encrypted data. It is particularly useful when the authorization policy for a master key allows one set of users to encrypt data and a different set of users to decrypt data.

The following table lists the variations of the recommended algorithm suites.

AWS Encryption SDK Algorithm Suites

Algorithm Name	Data Encryption Key Length (in bits)	Algorithm Mode	Key Derivation Algorithm	Signature Algorithm
AES	256	GCM	HKDF with SHA-384	ECDSA with P-384 and SHA-384
AES	192	GCM	HKDF with SHA-384	ECDSA with P-384 and SHA-384
AES	128	GCM	HKDF with SHA-256	ECDSA with P-256 and SHA-256

Other Supported Algorithm Suites

The AWS Encryption SDK supports the alternate algorithm suites for backward compatibility, although we do not recommend them. If you cannot use an algorithm suite with HKDF and signing, we recommend an algorithm suite with HKDF over one that lacks both elements.

AES-GCM with Key Derivation Only
This algorithm suite uses a key derivation function, but lacks the ECDSA signature that provides authenticity and nonrepudiation. Use this suite when the users who encrypt data and those who decrypt it are equally trusted.

AES-GCM without Key Derivation or Signing

This algorithm suite uses the data encryption key as the AES-GCM encryption key, instead of using a key derivation function to derive a unique key. We discourage using this suite to generate ciphertext, but the SDK supports it for compatibility reasons.

For more information about how these suites are represented and used in the library, see AWS Encryption SDK Algorithms Reference.

AWS Encryption SDK Programming Languages

The AWS Encryption SDK is available for the following programming languages. For more information, see the corresponding topic.

Topics

- Java
- Python
- Command Line Interface

AWS Encryption SDK for Java

This topic explains how to install and use the AWS Encryption SDK for Java. For details about programming with the SDK, see the aws-encryption-sdk-java repository on GitHub the Javadoc for the AWS Encryption SDK.

Topics

- Prerequisites
- Installation
- Example Code

Prerequisites

Before you install the AWS Encryption SDK for Java, be sure you have the following prerequisites.

A Java development environment
You will need Java 8 or later. On the Oracle website, go to Java SE Downloads, and then download and install the Java SE Development Kit (JDK).
If you use the Oracle JDK, you must also download and install the Java Cryptography Extension (JCE) Unlimited Strength Jurisdiction Policy Files.

Bouncy Castle
Bouncy Castle provides a cryptography API for Java. If you don't have Bouncy Castle, go to Bouncy Castle latest releases to download the provider file that corresponds to your JDK.
If you use Apache Maven, Bouncy Castle is available with the following dependency definition.

```
1 <dependency>
2   <groupId>org.bouncycastle</groupId>
3   <artifactId>bcprov-ext-jdk15on</artifactId>
4   <version>1.58</version>
5 </dependency>
```

AWS SDK for Java (Optional)
Although you don't need the AWS SDK for Java to use the AWS Encryption SDK for Java, you do need it to use AWS Key Management Service (AWS KMS) as a master key provider, and to use some of the example Java code in this guide. For more information about installing and configuring the AWS SDK for Java, see AWS SDK for Java.

Installation

You can install the AWS Encryption SDK for Java in the following ways.

Manually
To install the AWS Encryption SDK for Java, clone or download the aws-encryption-sdk-java GitHub repository.

Using Apache Maven
The AWS Encryption SDK for Java is available through Apache Maven with the following dependency definition.

```
1 <dependency>
2   <groupId>com.amazonaws</groupId>
3   <artifactId>aws-encryption-sdk-java</artifactId>
4   <version>1.3.1</version>
5 </dependency>
```

After you install the SDK, get started by looking at the example Java code in this guide and the Javadoc on GitHub.

AWS Encryption SDK for Java Example Code

The following examples show you how to use the AWS Encryption SDK for Java to encrypt and decrypt data.

Topics

- Strings
- Byte Streams
- Byte Streams with Multiple Master Key Providers

Encrypting and Decrypting Strings

The following example shows you how to use the AWS Encryption SDK to encrypt and decrypt strings.

This example uses an AWS Key Management Service (AWS KMS) customer master key (CMK) as the master key. For help creating a key, see Creating Keys in the *AWS Key Management Service Developer Guide.*

To find the Amazon Resource name (ARN) of an existing CMK, go to the **Encryption keys** section of the AWS Management Console, select the region, and then click the CMK alias. You can also use the AWS KMS ListKeys operation. For details, see Viewing Keys in the AWS Key Management Service Developer Guide.

```
1  /*
2   * Copyright 2017 Amazon.com, Inc. or its affiliates. All Rights Reserved.
3   *
4   * Licensed under the Apache License, Version 2.0 (the "License"). You may not use this file
        except
5   * in compliance with the License. A copy of the License is located at
6   *
7   * http://aws.amazon.com/apache2.0
8   *
9   * or in the "license" file accompanying this file. This file is distributed on an "AS IS" BASIS
        ,
10  * WITHOUT WARRANTIES OR CONDITIONS OF ANY KIND, either express or implied. See the License for
        the
11  * specific language governing permissions and limitations under the License.
12  */
13
14 package com.amazonaws.crypto.examples;
15
16 import java.util.Collections;
17 import java.util.Map;
18
19 import com.amazonaws.encryptionsdk.AwsCrypto;
20 import com.amazonaws.encryptionsdk.CryptoResult;
21 import com.amazonaws.encryptionsdk.kms.KmsMasterKey;
22 import com.amazonaws.encryptionsdk.kms.KmsMasterKeyProvider;
23
24 /**
25  * <p>
26  * Encrypts and then decrypts a string under a KMS key
27  *
28  * <p>
29  * Arguments:
30  * <ol>
31  * <li>Key ARN: For help finding the Amazon Resource Name (ARN) of your KMS customer master
```

```
32  *    key (CMK), see 'Viewing Keys' at http://docs.aws.amazon.com/kms/latest/developerguide/
           viewing-keys.html
33  * <li>String to encrypt
34  * </ol>
35  */
36  public class StringExample {
37      private static String keyArn;
38      private static String data;
39
40      public static void main(final String[] args) {
41          keyArn = args[0];
42          data = args[1];
43
44          // Instantiate the SDK
45          final AwsCrypto crypto = new AwsCrypto();
46
47          // Set up the KmsMasterKeyProvider backed by the default credentials
48          final KmsMasterKeyProvider prov = new KmsMasterKeyProvider(keyArn);
49
50          // Encrypt the data
51          //
52          // Most encrypted data should have an associated encryption context
53          // to protect integrity. This sample uses placeholder values.
54          //
55          // For more information see:
56          // blogs.aws.amazon.com/security/post/Tx2LZ6WBJJANTNW/How-to-Protect-the-Integrity-of-
                   Your-Encrypted-Data-by-Using-AWS-Key-Management
57          final Map<String, String> context = Collections.singletonMap("Example", "String");
58
59          final String ciphertext = crypto.encryptString(prov, data, context).getResult();
60          System.out.println("Ciphertext: " + ciphertext);
61
62          // Decrypt the data
63          final CryptoResult<String, KmsMasterKey> decryptResult = crypto.decryptString(prov,
                   ciphertext);
64
65          // Before returning the plaintext, verify that the customer master key that
66          // was used in the encryption operation was the one supplied to the master key provider.
67          if (!decryptResult.getMasterKeyIds().get(0).equals(keyArn)) {
68              throw new IllegalStateException("Wrong key ID!");
69          }
70
71          // Also, verify that the encryption context in the result contains the
72          // encryption context supplied to the encryptString method. Because the
73          // SDK can add values to the encryption context, don't require that
74          // the entire context matches.
75          for (final Map.Entry<String, String> e : context.entrySet()) {
76              if (!e.getValue().equals(decryptResult.getEncryptionContext().get(e.getKey()))) {
77                  throw new IllegalStateException("Wrong Encryption Context!");
78              }
79          }
80
81          // Now we can return the plaintext data
82          System.out.println("Decrypted: " + decryptResult.getResult());
```

```
83     }
84 }
```

Encrypting and Decrypting Byte Streams

The following example shows you how to use the AWS Encryption SDK to encrypt and decrypt byte streams. This example does not use AWS. It uses the Java Cryptography Extension (JCE) to protect the master key.

```
1  /*
2   * Copyright 2017 Amazon.com, Inc. or its affiliates. All Rights Reserved.
3   *
4   * Licensed under the Apache License, Version 2.0 (the "License"). You may not use this file
        except
5   * in compliance with the License. A copy of the License is located at
6   *
7   * http://aws.amazon.com/apache2.0
8   *
9   * or in the "license" file accompanying this file. This file is distributed on an "AS IS" BASIS
        ,
10  * WITHOUT WARRANTIES OR CONDITIONS OF ANY KIND, either express or implied. See the License for
        the
11  * specific language governing permissions and limitations under the License.
12  */
13
14 package com.amazonaws.crypto.examples;
15
16 import java.io.FileInputStream;
17 import java.io.FileOutputStream;
18 import java.io.IOException;
19 import java.security.SecureRandom;
20 import java.util.Collections;
21 import java.util.Map;
22
23 import javax.crypto.SecretKey;
24 import javax.crypto.spec.SecretKeySpec;
25
26 import com.amazonaws.encryptionsdk.AwsCrypto;
27 import com.amazonaws.encryptionsdk.CryptoInputStream;
28 import com.amazonaws.encryptionsdk.MasterKey;
29 import com.amazonaws.encryptionsdk.jce.JceMasterKey;
30 import com.amazonaws.util.IOUtils;
31
32 /**
33  * <p>
34  * Encrypts and then decrypts a file under a random key.
35  *
36  * <p>
37  * Arguments:
38  * <ol>
39  * <li>Name of file containing plaintext data to encrypt
40  * </ol>
41  *
42  * <p>
```

```java
43  * This program demonstrates using a standard Java {@link SecretKey} object as a {@link
       MasterKey} to
44  * encrypt and decrypt streaming data.
45  */
46  public class FileStreamingExample {
47      private static String srcFile;
48
49      public static void main(String[] args) throws IOException {
50          srcFile = args[0];
51
52          // In this example, we generate a random key. In practice,
53          // you would get a key from an existing store
54          SecretKey cryptoKey = retrieveEncryptionKey();
55
56          // Create a JCE master key provider using the random key and an AES-GCM encryption
                 algorithm
57          JceMasterKey masterKey = JceMasterKey.getInstance(cryptoKey, "Example", "RandomKey", "
             AES/GCM/NoPadding");
58
59          // Instantiate the SDK
60          AwsCrypto crypto = new AwsCrypto();
61
62          // Create an encryption context to identify this ciphertext
63          Map<String, String> context = Collections.singletonMap("Example", "FileStreaming");
64
65          // Because the file might be to large to load into memory, we stream the data, instead
                 of
66          //loading it all at once.
67          FileInputStream in = new FileInputStream(srcFile);
68          CryptoInputStream<JceMasterKey> encryptingStream = crypto.createEncryptingStream(
             masterKey, in, context);
69
70          FileOutputStream out = new FileOutputStream(srcFile + ".encrypted");
71          IOUtils.copy(encryptingStream, out);
72          encryptingStream.close();
73          out.close();
74
75          // Decrypt the file. Verify the encryption context before returning the plaintext.
76          in = new FileInputStream(srcFile + ".encrypted");
77          CryptoInputStream<JceMasterKey> decryptingStream = crypto.createDecryptingStream(
             masterKey, in);
78          // Does it contain the expected encryption context?
79          if (!"FileStreaming".equals(decryptingStream.getCryptoResult().getEncryptionContext().
             get("Example"))) {
80              throw new IllegalStateException("Bad encryption context");
81          }
82
83          // Return the plaintext data
84          out = new FileOutputStream(srcFile + ".decrypted");
85          IOUtils.copy(decryptingStream, out);
86          decryptingStream.close();
87          out.close();
88      }
89
```

```
90      /**
91       * In practice, this key would be saved in a secure location.
92       * For this demo, we generate a new random key for each operation.
93       */
94      private static SecretKey retrieveEncryptionKey() {
95          SecureRandom rnd = new SecureRandom();
96          byte[] rawKey = new byte[16]; // 128 bits
97          rnd.nextBytes(rawKey);
98          return new SecretKeySpec(rawKey, "AES");
99      }
100 }
```

Encrypting and Decrypting Byte Streams with Multiple Master Key Providers

The following example shows you how to use the AWS Encryption SDK with more than one master key provider. Using more than one master key provider creates redundancy if one master key provider is unavailable for decryption. This example uses a CMK in AWS KMS and an RSA key pair as the master keys.

```
1  /*
2   * Copyright 2017 Amazon.com, Inc. or its affiliates. All Rights Reserved.
3   *
4   * Licensed under the Apache License, Version 2.0 (the "License"). You may not use this file
         except
5   * in compliance with the License. A copy of the License is located at
6   *
7   * http://aws.amazon.com/apache2.0
8   *
9   * or in the "license" file accompanying this file. This file is distributed on an "AS IS" BASIS
         ,
10  * WITHOUT WARRANTIES OR CONDITIONS OF ANY KIND, either express or implied. See the License for
         the
11  * specific language governing permissions and limitations under the License.
12  */
13
14  package com.amazonaws.crypto.examples;
15
16  import java.io.FileInputStream;
17  import java.io.FileOutputStream;
18  import java.security.GeneralSecurityException;
19  import java.security.KeyPair;
20  import java.security.KeyPairGenerator;
21  import java.security.PrivateKey;
22  import java.security.PublicKey;
23
24  import com.amazonaws.encryptionsdk.AwsCrypto;
25  import com.amazonaws.encryptionsdk.CryptoOutputStream;
26  import com.amazonaws.encryptionsdk.MasterKeyProvider;
27  import com.amazonaws.encryptionsdk.jce.JceMasterKey;
28  import com.amazonaws.encryptionsdk.kms.KmsMasterKeyProvider;
29  import com.amazonaws.encryptionsdk.multi.MultipleProviderFactory;
30  import com.amazonaws.util.IOUtils;
31
32  /**
33   * <p>
```

```
34  * Encrypts a file using both KMS and an asymmetric key pair.
35  *
36  * <p>
37  * Arguments:
38  * <ol>
39  * <li>Key ARN: For help finding the Amazon Resource Name (ARN) of your KMS customer master
40  *    key (CMK), see 'Viewing Keys' at http://docs.aws.amazon.com/kms/latest/developerguide/
         viewing-keys.html
41  * <li>Name of file containing plaintext data to encrypt
42  * </ol>
43  *
44  * You might use AWS Key Management Service (KMS) for most encryption and decryption operations,
         but
45  * still want the option of decrypting your data offline independently of KMS. This sample
46  * demonstrates one way to do this.
47  *
48  * The sample encrypts data under both a KMS customer master key (CMK) and an "escrowed" RSA key
         pair
49  * so that either key alone can decrypt it. You might commonly use the KMS CMK for decryption.
         However,
50  * at any time, you can use the private RSA key to decrypt the ciphertext independent of KMS.
51  *
52  * This sample uses the JCEMasterKey class to generate a RSA public-private key pair
53  * and saves the key pair in memory. In practice, you would store the private key in a secure
         offline
54  * location, such as an offline HSM, and distribute the public key to your development team.
55  *
56  */
57  public class EscrowedEncryptExample {
58      private static PublicKey publicEscrowKey;
59      private static PrivateKey privateEscrowKey;
60
61      public static void main(final String[] args) throws Exception {
62          // This sample generates a new random key for each operation.
63          // In practice, you would distribute the public key and save the private key in secure
64          // storage.
65          generateEscrowKeyPair();
66
67          final String kmsArn = args[0];
68          final String fileName = args[1];
69
70          standardEncrypt(kmsArn, fileName);
71          standardDecrypt(kmsArn, fileName);
72
73          escrowDecrypt(fileName);
74      }
75
76      private static void standardEncrypt(final String kmsArn, final String fileName) throws
            Exception {
77          // Encrypt with the KMS CMK and the escrowed public key
78          // 1. Instantiate the SDK
79          final AwsCrypto crypto = new AwsCrypto();
80
81          // 2. Instantiate a KMS master key provider
```

```
82      final KmsMasterKeyProvider kms = new KmsMasterKeyProvider(kmsArn);

83

84      // 3. Instantiate a JCE master key provider
85      // Because the user does not have access to the private escrow key,
86      // they pass in "null" for the private key parameter.
87      final JceMasterKey escrowPub = JceMasterKey.getInstance(publicEscrowKey, null, "Escrow",
            "Escrow",
88          "RSA/ECB/OAEPWithSHA-512AndMGF1Padding");

89

90      // 4. Combine the providers into a single master key provider
91      final MasterKeyProvider<?> provider = MultipleProviderFactory.buildMultiProvider(kms,
            escrowPub);

92

93      // 5. Encrypt the file
94      // To simplify the code, we omit the encryption context. Production code should always
95      // use an encryption context. For an example, see the other SDK samples.
96      final FileInputStream in = new FileInputStream(fileName);
97      final FileOutputStream out = new FileOutputStream(fileName + ".encrypted");
98      final CryptoOutputStream<?> encryptingStream = crypto.createEncryptingStream(provider,
            out);

99

100     IOUtils.copy(in, encryptingStream);
101     in.close();
102     encryptingStream.close();
103 }

104

105 private static void standardDecrypt(final String kmsArn, final String fileName) throws
        Exception {
106     // Decrypt with the KMS CMK and the escrow public key. You can use a combined provider,
107     // as shown here, or just the KMS master key provider.

108

109     // 1. Instantiate the SDK
110     final AwsCrypto crypto = new AwsCrypto();

111

112     // 2. Instantiate a KMS master key provider
113     final KmsMasterKeyProvider kms = new KmsMasterKeyProvider(kmsArn);

114

115     // 3. Instantiate a JCE master key provider
116     // Because the user does not have access to the private escrow
117     // key, they pass in "null" for the private key parameter.
118     final JceMasterKey escrowPub = JceMasterKey.getInstance(publicEscrowKey, null, "Escrow",
            "Escrow",
119         "RSA/ECB/OAEPWithSHA-512AndMGF1Padding");

120

121     // 4. Combine the providers into a single master key provider
122     final MasterKeyProvider<?> provider = MultipleProviderFactory.buildMultiProvider(kms,
            escrowPub);

123

124     // 5. Decrypt the file
125     // To simplify the code, we omit the encryption context. Production code should always
126     // use an encryption context. For an example, see the other SDK samples.
127     final FileInputStream in = new FileInputStream(fileName + ".encrypted");
128     final FileOutputStream out = new FileOutputStream(fileName + ".decrypted");
```

```
129     final CryptoOutputStream<?> decryptingStream = crypto.createDecryptingStream(provider,
            out);
130     IOUtils.copy(in, decryptingStream);
131     in.close();
132     decryptingStream.close();
133   }
134
135   private static void escrowDecrypt(final String fileName) throws Exception {
136     // You can decrypt the stream using only the private key.
137     // This method does not call KMS.
138
139     // 1. Instantiate the SDK
140     final AwsCrypto crypto = new AwsCrypto();
141
142     // 2. Instantiate a JCE master key
143     // This method call uses the escrowed private key, not null
144     final JceMasterKey escrowPriv = JceMasterKey.getInstance(publicEscrowKey,
            privateEscrowKey, "Escrow", "Escrow",
145         "RSA/ECB/OAEPWithSHA-512AndMGF1Padding");
146
147     // 3. Decrypt the file
148      // To simplify the code, we omit the encryption context. Production code should always
149     // use an encryption context. For an example, see the other SDK samples.
150     final FileInputStream in = new FileInputStream(fileName + ".encrypted");
151     final FileOutputStream out = new FileOutputStream(fileName + ".deescrowed");
152     final CryptoOutputStream<?> decryptingStream = crypto.createDecryptingStream(escrowPriv,
            out);
153     IOUtils.copy(in, decryptingStream);
154     in.close();
155     decryptingStream.close();
156
157   }
158
159   private static void generateEscrowKeyPair() throws GeneralSecurityException {
160     final KeyPairGenerator kg = KeyPairGenerator.getInstance("RSA");
161     kg.initialize(4096); // Escrow keys should be very strong
162     final KeyPair keyPair = kg.generateKeyPair();
163     publicEscrowKey = keyPair.getPublic();
164     privateEscrowKey = keyPair.getPrivate();
165
166   }
167 }
```

AWS Encryption SDK for Python

This topic explains how to install and use the AWS Encryption SDK for Python. For details about programming with the SDK, see the aws-encryption-sdk-python repository on GitHub and the Python documentation for the AWS Encryption SDK for Python.

Topics

- Prerequisites
- Installation
- Example Code

Prerequisites

Before you install the AWS Encryption SDK for Python, be sure you have the following prerequisites.

A supported version of Python
To use this SDK, you need Python 2.7, or Python 3.3 or later. To download Python, see Python downloads.

The pip installation tool for Python
If you have Python 2.7.9 or later, or Python 3.4 or later, you already have pip, although you might want to upgrade it. For more information about upgrading or installing pip, see Installation in the pip documentation.

Installation

Use pip to install the AWS Encryption SDK for Python, as shown in the following examples.

To install the latest version

```
1 pip install aws-encryption-sdk
```

For more details about using pip to install and upgrade packages, see Installing Packages.

The SDK requires the cryptography library on all platforms. All versions of **pip** install and build the **cryptography** library on Windows. **pip** 8.1 and later installs and builds **cryptography** on Linux. If you are using an earlier version of **pip** and your Linux environment doesn't have the tools needed to build the **cryptography** library, you need to install them. For more information, see Building cryptography on Linux.

For the latest development version of this SDK, go to the aws-encryption-sdk-python GitHub repository.

After you install the SDK, get started by looking at the example Python code in this guide.

AWS Encryption SDK for Python Example Code

The following examples show you how to use the AWS Encryption SDK for Python to encrypt and decrypt data.

Topics

- Strings
- Byte Streams
- Byte Streams with Multiple Master Key Providers

Encrypting and Decrypting Strings

The following example shows you how to use the AWS Encryption SDK to encrypt and decrypt strings. This example uses a customer master key (CMK) in AWS Key Management Service (AWS KMS) as the master key.

```python
"""
Copyright 2017 Amazon.com, Inc. or its affiliates. All Rights Reserved.

Licensed under the Apache License, Version 2.0 (the "License"). You may not use this file except
in compliance with the License. A copy of the License is located at

https://aws.amazon.com/apache-2-0/

or in the "license" file accompanying this file. This file is distributed on an "AS IS" BASIS,
WITHOUT WARRANTIES OR CONDITIONS OF ANY KIND, either express or implied. See the License for the
specific language governing permissions and limitations under the License.
"""

from __future__ import print_function

import aws_encryption_sdk


def cycle_string(key_arn, source_plaintext, botocore_session=None):
    """Encrypts and then decrypts a string using a KMS customer master key (CMK)

    :param str key_arn: Amazon Resource Name (ARN) of the KMS CMK
    (http://docs.aws.amazon.com/kms/latest/developerguide/viewing-keys.html)
    :param bytes source_plaintext: Data to encrypt
    :param botocore_session: Existing Botocore session instance
    :type botocore_session: botocore.session.Session
    """

    # Create a KMS master key provider
    kms_kwargs = dict(key_ids=[key_arn])
    if botocore_session is not None:
        kms_kwargs['botocore_session'] = botocore_session
    master_key_provider = aws_encryption_sdk.KMSMasterKeyProvider(**kms_kwargs)

    # Encrypt the plaintext source data
    ciphertext, encryptor_header = aws_encryption_sdk.encrypt(
        source=source_plaintext,
        key_provider=master_key_provider
    )
    print('Ciphertext: ', ciphertext)
```

```
41
42     # Decrypt the ciphertext
43     cycled_plaintext, decrypted_header = aws_encryption_sdk.decrypt(
44         source=ciphertext,
45         key_provider=master_key_provider
46     )
47
48     # Verify that the "cycled" (encrypted, then decrypted) plaintext is identical to the source
49     # plaintext
50     assert cycled_plaintext == source_plaintext
51
52     # Verify that the encryption context used in the decrypt operation includes all key pairs
           from
53     # the encrypt operation. (The SDK can add pairs, so don't require an exact match.)
54     #
55     # In production, always use a meaningful encryption context. In this sample, we omit the
56     # encryption context (no key pairs).
57     assert all(
58         pair in decrypted_header.encryption_context.items()
59         for pair in encryptor_header.encryption_context.items()
60     )
61
62     print('Decrypted: ', cycled_plaintext)
```

Encrypting and Decrypting Byte Streams

The following example shows you how to use the AWS Encryption SDK to encrypt and decrypt byte streams. This example doesn't use AWS. It uses a static, ephemeral master key provider.

```
1  """
2  Copyright 2017 Amazon.com, Inc. or its affiliates. All Rights Reserved.
3
4  Licensed under the Apache License, Version 2.0 (the "License"). You may not use this file except
5  in compliance with the License. A copy of the License is located at
6
7  https://aws.amazon.com/apache-2-0/
8
9  or in the "license" file accompanying this file. This file is distributed on an "AS IS" BASIS,
10 WITHOUT WARRANTIES OR CONDITIONS OF ANY KIND, either express or implied. See the License for the
11 specific language governing permissions and limitations under the License.
12 """
13
14 import filecmp
15 import os
16
17 import aws_encryption_sdk
18 from aws_encryption_sdk.internal.crypto import WrappingKey
19 from aws_encryption_sdk.key_providers.raw import RawMasterKeyProvider
20 from aws_encryption_sdk.identifiers import WrappingAlgorithm, EncryptionKeyType
21
22
23 class StaticRandomMasterKeyProvider(RawMasterKeyProvider):
24     """Randomly and consistently generates 256-bit keys for each unique key ID."""
25     provider_id = 'static-random'
```

```
26
27   def __init__(self, **kwargs):
28       self._static_keys = {}
29
30   def _get_raw_key(self, key_id):
31       """Returns a static, randomly-generated symmetric key for the specified key ID.
32
33       :param str key_id: Key ID
34       :returns: Wrapping key that contains the specified static key
35       :rtype: :class:`aws_encryption_sdk.internal.crypto.WrappingKey`
36       """
37       try:
38           static_key = self._static_keys[key_id]
39       except KeyError:
40           static_key = os.urandom(32)
41           self._static_keys[key_id] = static_key
42       return WrappingKey(
43           wrapping_algorithm=WrappingAlgorithm.AES_256_GCM_IV12_TAG16_NO_PADDING,
44           wrapping_key=static_key,
45           wrapping_key_type=EncryptionKeyType.SYMMETRIC
46       )
47
48
49  def cycle_file(source_plaintext_filename):
50      """Encrypts and then decrypts a file under a custom static master key provider.
51
52      :param str source_plaintext_filename: Filename of file to encrypt
53      """
54
55      # Create a static random master key provider
56      key_id = os.urandom(8)
57      master_key_provider = StaticRandomMasterKeyProvider()
58      master_key_provider.add_master_key(key_id)
59
60      ciphertext_filename = source_plaintext_filename + '.encrypted'
61      cycled_plaintext_filename = source_plaintext_filename + '.decrypted'
62
63      # Encrypt the plaintext source data
64      with open(source_plaintext_filename, 'rb') as plaintext, open(ciphertext_filename, 'wb') as
65          ciphertext:
66          with aws_encryption_sdk.stream(
67              mode='e',
68              source=plaintext,
69              key_provider=master_key_provider
70          ) as encryptor:
71              for chunk in encryptor:
72                  ciphertext.write(chunk)
73
74      # Decrypt the ciphertext
75      with open(ciphertext_filename, 'rb') as ciphertext, open(cycled_plaintext_filename, 'wb') as
76          plaintext:
77          with aws_encryption_sdk.stream(
78              mode='d',
79              source=ciphertext,
```

```
78              key_provider=master_key_provider
79          ) as decryptor:
80              for chunk in decryptor:
81                  plaintext.write(chunk)
82
83      # Verify that the "cycled" (encrypted, then decrypted) plaintext is identical to the source
84      # plaintext
85      assert filecmp.cmp(source_plaintext_filename, cycled_plaintext_filename)
86
87      # Verify that the encryption context used in the decrypt operation includes all key pairs
           from
88      # the encrypt operation
89          #
90      # In production, always use a meaningful encryption context. In this sample, we omit the
91      # encryption context (no key pairs).
92      assert all(
93          pair in decryptor.header.encryption_context.items()
94          for pair in encryptor.header.encryption_context.items()
95      )
96      return ciphertext_filename, cycled_plaintext_filename
```

Encrypting and Decrypting Byte Streams with Multiple Master Key Providers

The following example shows you how to use the AWS Encryption SDK with more than one master key provider. Using more than one master key provider creates redundancy if one master key provider is unavailable for decryption. This example uses a CMK in AWS KMS and an RSA key pair as the master keys.

```
1  """
2  Copyright 2017 Amazon.com, Inc. or its affiliates. All Rights Reserved.
3
4  Licensed under the Apache License, Version 2.0 (the "License"). You may not use this file except
5  in compliance with the License. A copy of the License is located at
6
7  https://aws.amazon.com/apache-2-0/
8
9  or in the "license" file accompanying this file. This file is distributed on an "AS IS" BASIS,
10 WITHOUT WARRANTIES OR CONDITIONS OF ANY KIND, either express or implied. See the License for the
11 specific language governing permissions and limitations under the License.
12 """
13
14 import filecmp
15 import os
16
17 import aws_encryption_sdk
18 from aws_encryption_sdk.internal.crypto import WrappingKey
19 from aws_encryption_sdk.key_providers.raw import RawMasterKeyProvider
20 from aws_encryption_sdk.identifiers import WrappingAlgorithm, EncryptionKeyType
21 from cryptography.hazmat.backends import default_backend
22 from cryptography.hazmat.primitives import serialization
23 from cryptography.hazmat.primitives.asymmetric import rsa
24
25
26 class StaticRandomMasterKeyProvider(RawMasterKeyProvider):
27     provider_id = 'static-random'
```

```
28
29    def __init__(self, **kwargs):
30        self._static_keys = {}
31
32    def _get_raw_key(self, key_id):
33        """Returns a static, randomly generated, RSA key for the specified key ID.
34
35        :param str key_id: User-defined ID for the static key
36        :returns: Wrapping key that contains the specified static key
37        :rtype: :class:`aws_encryption_sdk.internal.crypto.WrappingKey`
38        """
39        try:
40            static_key = self._static_keys[key_id]
41        except KeyError:
42            private_key = rsa.generate_private_key(
43                public_exponent=65537,
44                key_size=4096,
45                backend=default_backend()
46            )
47            static_key = private_key.private_bytes(
48                encoding=serialization.Encoding.PEM,
49                format=serialization.PrivateFormat.PKCS8,
50                encryption_algorithm=serialization.NoEncryption()
51            )
52            self._static_keys[key_id] = static_key
53        return WrappingKey(
54            wrapping_algorithm=WrappingAlgorithm.RSA_OAEP_SHA1_MGF1,
55            wrapping_key=static_key,
56            wrapping_key_type=EncryptionKeyType.PRIVATE
57        )
58
59
60 def cycle_file(key_arn, source_plaintext_filename, botocore_session=None):
61     """Encrypts and then decrypts a file using a KMS master key provider and a custom static
           master
62     key provider. Both master key providers are used to encrypt the plaintext file, so either
           one alone
63     can decrypt it.
64
65     :param str key_arn: Amazon Resource Name (ARN) of the KMS Customer Master Key (CMK) (http://
           docs.aws.amazon.com/kms/latest/developerguide/viewing-keys.html)
66     :param str source_plaintext_filename: Filename of file to encrypt
67     :param botocore_session: existing botocore session instance
68     :type botocore_session: botocore.session.Session
69     """
70
71     # "Cycled" means encrypted and then decrypted
72     ciphertext_filename = source_plaintext_filename + '.encrypted'
73     cycled_kms_plaintext_filename = source_plaintext_filename + '.kms.decrypted'
74     cycled_static_plaintext_filename = source_plaintext_filename + '.static.decrypted'
75
76     # Create a KMS master key provider
77     kms_kwargs = dict(key_ids=[key_arn])
78     if botocore_session is not None:
```

```
79        kms_kwargs['botocore_session'] = botocore_session
80    kms_master_key_provider = aws_encryption_sdk.KMSMasterKeyProvider(**kms_kwargs)
81
82    # Create a static master key provider and add a master key to it
83    static_key_id = os.urandom(8)
84    static_master_key_provider = StaticRandomMasterKeyProvider()
85    static_master_key_provider.add_master_key(static_key_id)
86
87    # Create a master key provider that includes the KMS and static master key providers
88    kms_master_key_provider.add_master_key_provider(static_master_key_provider)
89
90    # Encrypt plaintext with both KMS and static master keys
91    with open(source_plaintext_filename, 'rb') as plaintext, open(ciphertext_filename, 'wb') as
          ciphertext:
92        with aws_encryption_sdk.stream(
93            source=plaintext,
94            mode='e',
95            key_provider=kms_master_key_provider
96        ) as encryptor:
97            for chunk in encryptor:
98                ciphertext.write(chunk)
99
100   # Decrypt the ciphertext with only the KMS master key
101   with open(ciphertext_filename, 'rb') as ciphertext, open(cycled_kms_plaintext_filename, 'wb
          ') as plaintext:
102       with aws_encryption_sdk.stream(
103           source=ciphertext,
104           mode='d',
105           key_provider=aws_encryption_sdk.KMSMasterKeyProvider(**kms_kwargs)
106       ) as kms_decryptor:
107           for chunk in kms_decryptor:
108               plaintext.write(chunk)
109
110   # Decrypt the ciphertext with only the static master key
111   with open(ciphertext_filename, 'rb') as ciphertext, open(cycled_static_plaintext_filename, '
          wb') as plaintext:
112       with aws_encryption_sdk.stream(
113           source=ciphertext,
114           mode='d',
115           key_provider=static_master_key_provider
116       ) as static_decryptor:
117           for chunk in static_decryptor:
118               plaintext.write(chunk)
119
120   # Verify that the "cycled" (encrypted, then decrypted) plaintext is identical to the source
121   # plaintext
122   assert filecmp.cmp(source_plaintext_filename, cycled_kms_plaintext_filename)
123   assert filecmp.cmp(source_plaintext_filename, cycled_static_plaintext_filename)
124
125   # Verify that the encryption context in the decrypt operation includes all key pairs from
          the
126   # encrypt operation.
127   #
128   # In production, always use a meaningful encryption context. In this sample, we omit the
```

```
129    # encryption context (no key pairs).
130    assert all(
131        pair in kms_decryptor.header.encryption_context.items()
132        for pair in encryptor.header.encryption_context.items()
133    )
134    assert all(
135        pair in static_decryptor.header.encryption_context.items()
136        for pair in encryptor.header.encryption_context.items()
137    )
138    return ciphertext_filename, cycled_kms_plaintext_filename, cycled_static_plaintext_filename
```

AWS Encryption SDK Command Line Interface

The AWS Encryption SDK Command Line Interface (AWS Encryption CLI) enables you to use the AWS Encryption SDK to encrypt and decrypt data interactively at the command line and in scripts. You don't need cryptography or programming expertise.

Like all implementations of the AWS Encryption SDK, the AWS Encryption CLI offers advanced data protection features. These include envelope encryption, additional authenticated data (AAD), and secure, authenticated, symmetric key algorithm suites, such as 256-bit AES-GCM with key derivation and signing.

The AWS Encryption CLI is built on the AWS Encryption SDK for Python and is supported on Linux, macOS, and Windows. You can run commands and scripts to encrypt and decrypt your data in your preferred shell on Linux or macOS, in a Command Prompt window (cmd.exe) on Windows, and in a PowerShell console on any system.

All language-specific implementations of the AWS Encryption SDK, including the AWS Encryption CLI, are interoperable. For example, you can encrypt data with the AWS Encryption SDK for Java and decrypt it with the AWS Encryption CLI.

This topic introduces the AWS Encryption CLI, explains how to install and use it, and provides several examples to help you get started. For a quick start, see How to Encrypt and Decrypt Your Data with the AWS Encryption CLI in the AWS Security Blog. For more detailed information, see Read The Docs, and join us in developing the AWS Encryption CLI in the aws-encryption-sdk-cli repository on GitHub.

Topics

- Installing the CLI
- How to Use the CLI
- Examples
- Syntax and Parameter Reference

Installing the AWS Encryption SDK Command Line Interface

This topic explains how to install the AWS Encryption CLI. For detailed information, see the aws-encryption-sdk-cli repository on GitHub and Read the Docs.

Topics

- Installing the Prerequisites
- Installing the AWS Encryption CLI

Installing the Prerequisites

The AWS Encryption CLI is built on the AWS Encryption SDK for Python. To use the AWS Encryption CLI, you need Python and **pip**, the Python package management tool. Python and **pip** are available on all supported platforms.

Before you install the AWS Encryption CLI, be sure that you have the following prerequisites.

Python
The AWS Encryption CLI requires Python 2.7, or Python 3.4 or later. Python is included in most Linux and macOS installations, although you might need to upgrade to one of the required versions. However, you have to install Python on Windows, if it is not already installed. To download Python, see Python downloads.
To determine whether Python is installed, at the command line, type:

```
1 python
```

To check the Python version, use the -V (uppercase V) parameter.

```
1 python -V
```

On Windows, you need to install Python. Then, add the path to the `Python.exe` file to the value of the **Path** environment variable.
By default, Python is installed in the all users directory or in a user profile directory (`$home` or `%userprofile%`) in the `AppData\Local\Programs\Python` subdirectory. To find the location of the `Python.exe` file on your system, check one of the following registry keys. You can use PowerShell to search the registry.

```
1 PS C:\> dir HKLM:\Software\Python\PythonCore\version\InstallPath
2 # -or-
3 PS C:\> dir HKCU:\Software\Python\PythonCore\version\InstallPath
```

pip
pip is the Python package manager. To install the AWS Encryption CLI and its dependencies, you need **pip** 8.1 or later.
For help installing or upgrading **pip**, see Installation in the **pip** documentation.

AWS Command Line Interface
The AWS Command Line Interface (AWS CLI) is required only if you are using AWS Key Management Service (AWS KMS) customer master keys (CMKs) with the AWS Encryption CLI. If you are using a different master key provider, the AWS CLI is not required.
To use AWS KMS CMKs with the AWS Encryption CLI, you need to install and configure the AWS CLI. The configuration makes the credentials that you use to authenticate to AWS KMS available to the AWS Encryption CLI.

Installing the AWS Encryption CLI

Use **pip** to install the AWS Encryption CLI and the Python cryptography library that it requires.

The AWS Encryption CLI requires the **cryptography** library on all platforms. All versions of **pip** install and build the **cryptography** library on Windows and OS X.

On Linux, **pip** 8.1 and later installs and builds the **cryptography** library. If you are using an earlier version of **pip** and your Linux environment doesn't have the tools needed to build the **cryptography** library, you must install them. For more information, see Building cryptography on Linux.

To install the latest version

```
1 pip install aws-encryption-sdk-cli
```

To upgrade to the latest version

```
1 pip install --upgrade aws-encryption-sdk-cli
```

To find the version number of your AWS Encryption CLI and AWS Encryption SDK

```
1 aws-encryption-cli --version
2
3 aws-encryption-sdk-cli/1.1.0 aws-encryption-sdk/1.3.2
```

To install the version of the AWS Encryption CLI currently in development, see the aws-encryption-sdk-cli repository on GitHub.

For more details about using **pip** to install and upgrade Python packages, see the pip documentation.

How to Use the AWS Encryption SDK Command Line Interface

This topic explains how to use the parameters in the AWS Encryption CLI. For examples, see Examples of the AWS Encryption SDK Command Line Interface. For complete documentation, see Read the Docs.

Topics

- How to Encrypt and Decrypt Data
- How to Specify a Master Key
- How to Provide Input
- How to Specify the Output Location
- How to Use an Encryption Context
- How to Store Parameters in a Configuration File

How to Encrypt and Decrypt Data

The AWS Encryption CLI uses the features of the AWS Encryption SDK to make it easy to encrypt and decrypt data securely.

- When you encrypt data in the AWS Encryption CLI, you specify your plaintext data and a master key, such as an AWS Key Management Service (AWS KMS) customer master key (CMK). If you are using a custom master key provider, you need to specify the provider. You also specify output locations for the encrypted message and for metadata about the encryption operation. An encryption context is optional, but recommended.

```
1 aws-encryption-cli --encrypt --input myPlaintextData \
2                    --master-keys key=1234abcd-12ab-34cd-56ef-1234567890ab \
3                    --output myEncryptedMessage \
4                    --metadata-output ~/metadata \
5                    --encryption-context purpose=test
```

  The AWS Encryption CLI gets a unique data key from the master key and encrypts your data. It returns an encrypted message and metadata about the operation. The encrypted message contains your encrypted data (*ciphertext*) and an encrypted copy of the data key. You don't have to worry about storing, managing, or losing the data key.

- When you decrypt data, you pass in your encrypted message, the optional encryption context, and location for the plaintext output and the metadata. If you are using a custom master key provider, you also supply the master key. If you are using an AWS KMS CMK, AWS KMS derives the master key from the encrypted message.

```
1 aws-encryption-cli --decrypt --input myEncryptedMessage \
2                    --output myPlaintextData \
3                    --metadata-output ~/metadata \
4                    --encryption-context purpose=test
```

  The AWS Encryption CLI uses the master key to decrypt the data key in the encrypted message. Then it uses the data key to decrypt your data. It returns your plaintext data and metadata about the operation.

How to Specify a Master Key

When you encrypt data in the AWS Encryption CLI, you need to specify a master key. You can use an AWS KMS customer master key (CMK) or a master key from a custom master key provider. The custom master key provider can be any compatible Python master key provider.

39

To specify a master key, use the `--master-keys` parameter (`-m`). Its value is a collection of attributes with the `attribute=value` format. The attributes that you use depend on the master key provider and the command.

- **AWS KMS**. In encrypt commands, you must specify a `--master-keys` parameter with a **key** attribute. The other attributes are optional. In decrypt commands, the `--master-keys` parameter is optional and it can only have a **profile** attribute.
- **Custom master key provider**. You must specify the `--master-keys` parameter in every command. The parameter value must have **key** and **provider** attributes.

You can include multiple `--master-keys` parameters in the same command.

Master Key Parameter Attributes

The value of the `--master-keys` parameter consists of the following attributes and their values.

If an attribute name or value includes spaces or special characters, enclose both the name and value in quotation marks. For example, `--master-keys key=12345 "provider=my cool provider"`.

Key: Specify a Master Key
Use the **key** attribute to identify a master key. The value can be any key identifier that the master key provider recognizes.

```
1  --master-keys key=1234abcd-12ab-34cd-56ef-1234567890ab
```

In an encrypt command, each `--master-keys` parameter value must include at least one **key** attribute and value. You can use multiple **key** attributes in each `--master-keys` parameter value.

```
1  aws-encryption-cli --encrypt --master-keys key=1234abcd-12ab-34cd-56ef-1234567890ab key=1a2b3c4d
     -5e6f-1a2b-3c4d-5e6f1a2b3c4d
```

In encrypt commands that use AWS KMS CMKs, the value of **key** can be the CMK ID, its Amazon Resource Name (ARN), an alias name, or alias ARN. For example, this encrypt command uses an alias ARN in the value of the **key** attribute.

```
1  aws-encryption-cli --encrypt --master-keys key=arn:aws:kms:us-west-2:111122223333:alias/
     ExampleAlias
```

In decrypt commands that use a custom master key provider, **key** and **provider** attributes are required. The key attribute is not permitted in decrypt commands that use an AWS KMS CMK.

```
1  aws-encryption-cli --decrypt --master-keys provider='myProvider' key='100101'
```

Provider: Specify the Master Key Provider
The **provider** attribute identifies the master key provider. The default value is `aws-kms`, which represents AWS KMS. If you are using a different master key provider, the **provider** attribute is required.

```
1  --master-keys key=12345 provider=my_custom_provider
```

For more information about using custom (non-AWS KMS) master key providers, see the **Advanced Configuration** topic in the README file for the AWS Encryption SDK CLI repository.

Region: Specify an AWS Region
Use the **region** attribute to specify the AWS Region of an AWS KMS CMK. This attribute is valid only in encrypt commands and only when the master key provider is AWS KMS.

```
1  --encrypt --master-keys key=alias/primary-key region=us-east-2
```

AWS Encryption CLI commands use the AWS Region that is specified in the **key** attribute value if it includes a region, such as an ARN. if the **key** value specifies a AWS Region, the **region** attribute is ignored.
The **region** attribute takes precedence over other region specifications. If you don't use a region attribute, AWS

Encryption CLI commands uses the AWS Region specified in your AWS CLI named profile, if any, or your default profile.

Profile: Specify a Named Profile

Use the **profile** attribute to specify an AWS CLI named profile. Named profiles can include credentials and an AWS Region. This attribute is valid only when the master key provider is AWS KMS.

```
1 --master-keys key=alias/primary-key profile=admin-1
```

You can use the **profile** attribute to specify alternate credentials in encrypt and decrypt commands. In an encrypt command, the AWS Encryption CLI uses the AWS Region in the named profile only when the **key** value does not include a region and there is no **region** attribute. In a decrypt command, the AWS Region in the name profile is ignored.

How to Specify Multiple Master Keys

You can specify multiple master keys in each command.

If you specify more than one master key, the first master key generates (and encrypts) the data key that is used to encrypt your data. The other master keys only encrypt the data key. The resulting encrypted message contains the encrypted data ("ciphertext") and a collection of encrypted data keys, one encrypted by each master key. Any of the master keys can decrypt one data key and then decrypt the data.

There are two ways to specify multiple master keys:

- Include multiple **key** attributes in a --master-keys parameter value.

```
1 $cmk_oregon=arn:aws:kms:us-west-2:111122223333:key/1234abcd-12ab-34cd-56ef-1234567890ab
2 $cmk_ohio=arn:aws:kms:us-east-2:111122223333:key/0987ab65-43cd-21ef-09ab-87654321cdef
3
4 --master-keys key=$cmk_oregon key=$cmk_ohio
```

- Include multiple --master-keys parameters in the same command. Use this syntax when the attribute values that you specify do not apply to all of the master keys in the command.

```
1 --master-keys region=us-east-2 key=alias/primary_CMK \
2 --master-keys region=us-west-1 key=alias/primary_CMK
```

How to Provide Input

The encrypt operation in the AWS Encryption CLI takes plaintext data as input and returns an encrypted message. The decrypt operation takes an encrypted message as input and returns plaintext data.

The --input parameter (-i) , which tells the AWS Encryption CLI where to find the input, is required in all AWS Encryption CLI commands.

You can provide input in any of the following ways:

- Use a file.

```
1 --input myData.txt
```

- Use a file name pattern.

```
1 --input testdir/*.xml
```

- Use a directory or directory name pattern. When the input is a directory, the --recursive parameter (-r, -R) is required.

```
1 --input testdir --recursive
```

- Pipe input to the command (stdin). Use a value of - for the --input parameter. (The --input parameter is always required.)

```
1 echo 'Hello World' | aws-encryption-cli --encrypt --input -
```

How to Specify the Output Location

The --output parameter tells the AWS Encryption CLI where to write the results of the encryption or decryption operation. It is required in every AWS Encryption CLI command. The AWS Encryption CLI creates a new output file for every input file in the operation.

If an output file already exists, by default, the AWS Encryption CLI prints a warning, then overwrites the file. To prevent overwriting, use the --interactive parameter, which prompts you for confirmation before overwriting, or --no-overwrite, which skips the input if the output would cause an overwrite. To suppress the overwrite warning, use --quiet. To capture errors and warnings from the AWS Encryption CLI, use the 2>&1 redirection operator to write them to the output stream.

Note
Commands that overwrite output files begin by deleting the output file. If the command fails, the output file might already be deleted.

You can the output location in several ways.

- Specify a file name. If you specify a path to the file, all directories in the path must exist before the command runs.

```
1 --output myEncryptedData.txt
```

- Specify a directory. The output directory must exist before the command runs.

  If the input contains subdirectories, the command reproduces the subdirectories under the specified directory.

```
1 --output Test
```

  When the output location is a directory (without file names), the AWS Encryption CLI creates output file names based on the input file names plus a suffix. Encrypt operations append .encrypted to the input file name and the decrypt operations append .decrypted. To change the suffix, use the --suffix parameter.

  For example, if you encrypt file.txt, the encrypt command creates file.txt.encrypted. If you decrypt file.txt.encrypted, the decrypt command creates file.txt.encrypted.decrypted.

- Write to the command line (stdout). Enter a value of - for the --output parameter. You can use --output - to pipe output to another command or program.

```
1 --output -
```

How to Use an Encryption Context

The AWS Encryption CLI lets you provide an encryption context in encrypt and decrypt commands. It is not required, but it is a cryptographic best practice that we recommend.

An *encryption context* is a type of arbitrary, non-secret *additional authenticated data*. In the AWS Encryption CLI, the encryption context consists of a collection of name=value pairs. You can use any content in the pairs,

42

including information about the files, data that helps you to find the encryption operation in logs, or data that your grants or policies require.

In an Encrypt Command

The encryption context that you specify in an encrypt command, along with any additional encryption context that the encryption components add, is cryptographically bound to the encrypted data. It is also included (in plaintext) in the encrypted message that the command returns. If you are using an AWS KMS customer master key (CMK), the encryption context also might appear in plaintext in audit records and logs, such as AWS CloudTrail.

The following example shows a encryption context with three `name=value` pairs.

```
1 --encryption-context purpose=test dept=IT class=confidential
```

In a Decrypt Command

In a decrypt command, the encryption context helps you to confirm that you are decrypting the right encrypted message.

You are not required to provide an encryption context in a decrypt command, even if an encryption context was used on encrypt. However, if you do, the AWS Encryption CLI verifies that every element in the encryption context of the decrypt command matches an element in the encryption context of the encrypted message. If any element does not match, the decrypt command fails.

For example, the following command decrypts the encrypted message only if its encryption context includes `dept=IT`.

```
1 aws-encryption-cli --decrypt --encryption-context dept=IT ...
```

An encryption context is an important part of your security strategy. However, when choosing an encryption context, remember that its values are not secret. Do not include any confidential data in the encryption context.

To specify an encryption context:

- In an **encrypt** command, use the `--encryption-context` parameter with one or more `name=value` pairs. Use a space to separate each pair.

```
1 --encryption-context name=value [name=value] ...
```

- In a **decrypt** command, the `--encryption-context` parameter value can include `name=value` pairs, `name` elements (with no values), or a combination of both.

```
1 --encryption-context name[=value] [name] [name=value] ...
```

If the `name` or `value` in a `name=value` pair includes spaces or special characters, enclose the entire pair in quotation marks.

```
1 --encryption-context "department=software engineering" "AWS Region=us-west-2"
```

For example, this encrypt command includes an encryption context with two pairs, `purpose=test` and `dept=23`.

```
1 aws-encryption-cli --encrypt --encryption-context purpose=test dept=23 ...
```

These decrypt command would succeed. The encryption context in each commands is a subset of the original encryption context.

```
1 \\ Any one or both of the encryption context pairs
2 aws-encryption-cli --decrypt --encryption-context dept=23 ...
3
4 \\ Any one or both of the encryption context names
5 aws-encryption-cli --decrypt --encryption-context purpose ...
```

```
6
7 \\ Any combination of names and pairs
8 aws-encryption-cli --decrypt --encryption-context dept purpose=test ...
```

However, these decrypt commands would fail. The encryption context in the encrypted message does not contain the specified elements.

```
1 aws-encryption-cli --decrypt --encryption-context dept=Finance ...
2 aws-encryption-cli --decrypt --encryption-context scope ...
```

How to Store Parameters in a Configuration File

You can save time and avoid typing errors by saving frequently used AWS Encryption CLI parameters and values in configuration files.

A *configuration file* is a text file that contains parameters and values for an AWS Encryption CLI command. When you refer to a configuration file in a AWS Encryption CLI command, the reference is replaced by the parameters and values in the configuration file. The effect is the same is if you typed the file content at the command line. A configuration file can have any name and it can be located in any directory that the current user can access.

The following example configuration file, `cmk.conf`, specifies two AWS KMS CMKs in different regions.

```
1 --master-keys key=arn:aws:kms:us-west-2:111122223333:key/1234abcd-12ab-34cd-56ef-1234567890ab
2 --master-keys key=arn:aws:kms:us-east-2:111122223333:key/0987ab65-43cd-21ef-09ab-87654321cdef
```

To use the configuration file in a command, prefix the file name with an at sign (@). In a PowerShell console, use a backtick character to escape the at sign ("@`").

This example command uses the `cmk.conf` file in an encrypt command.

[Bash]

```
1 $ aws-encryption-cli -e @cmk.conf -i hello.txt -o testdir
```

[PowerShell]

```
1 PS C:\> aws-encryption-cli -e `@cmk.conf -i .\Hello.txt -o .\TestDir
```

Configuration File Rules

The rules for using configuration files are as follows:

- You can include multiple parameters in each configuration file and list them in any order. List each parameter with its values (if any) on a separate line.
- Use # to add a comment to all or part of a line.
- You can include references to other configuration files. Do not use a backtick to escape the @ sign, even in PowerShell.
- If you use quotes in a configuration file, the quoted text cannot span multiple lines.

For example, this is the contents of an example `encrypt.conf` file.

```
1 # Archive Files
2 --encrypt
3 --output /archive/logs
4 --recursive
5 --interactive
6 --encryption-context class=unclassified dept=IT
7 --suffix  # No suffix
8 --metadata-output ~/metadata
9 @caching.conf  # Use limited caching
```

You can also include multiple configuration files in a command. This example command uses both the `encrypt.conf` and `master-keys.conf` configurations files.

[Bash]

```
1 $  aws-encryption-cli -i /usr/logs @encrypt.conf @master-keys.conf
```

[PowerShell]

```
1 PS C:\> aws-encryption-cli -i $home\Test\*.log `@encrypt.conf `@master-keys.conf
```

**Next: **Try the AWS Encryption CLI examples

Examples of the AWS Encryption SDK Command Line Interface

Use the following examples to try the AWS Encryption CLI on the platform you prefer. For help with master keys and other parameters, see How to Use the AWS Encryption SDK Command Line Interface. For a quick reference, see AWS Encryption SDK CLI Syntax and Parameter Reference.

Topics

- Encrypting a File
- Decrypting a File
- Encrypting All Files in a Directory
- Decrypting All Files in a Directory
- Encrypting and Decrypting on the Command Line
- Using Multiple Master Keys
- Encrypting and Decrypting in Scripts
- Using Data Key Caching

Encrypting a File

This example uses the AWS Encryption CLI to encrypt the contents of the `hello.txt` file, which contains a "Hello World" string.

When you run an encrypt command on a file, the AWS Encryption CLI gets the contents of the file, generates a unique data key, encrypts the file contents under the data key, and then writes the encrypted message to a new file.

The first command saves the Amazon Resource Name (ARN) of an AWS KMS customer master key (CMK) in the `$cmkArn` variable.

The second command encrypts the file contents. The command uses the `--encrypt` parameter to specify the operation and the `--input` parameter to indicate the file to encrypt. The `--master-keys` parameter, and its required **key** attribute, tell the command to use the master key represented by the CMK ARN.

The command uses the `--metadata-output` parameter to specify a text file for the metadata about the encryption operation. As a best practice, the command uses the `--encryption-context` parameter to specify an encryption context.

The value of the `--output` parameter, a dot (.), tells the command to write the output file to the current directory.

[**Bash**]

```
1 \\ To run this example, replace the fictitious CMK ARN with a valid value.
2 $ cmkArn=arn:aws:kms:us-west-2:111122223333:key/1234abcd-12ab-34cd-56ef-1234567890ab
3
4 $ aws-encryption-cli --encrypt \
5                      --input hello.txt \
6                      --master-keys key=$cmkArn \
7                      --metadata-output ~/metadata \
8                      --encryption-context purpose=test \
9                      --output .
```

[PowerShell]

```
1 # To run this example, replace the fictitious CMK ARN with a valid value.
2 PS C:\> $CmkArn = arn:aws:kms:us-west-2:111122223333:key/1234abcd-12ab-34cd-56ef-1234567890ab
3
4 PS C:\> aws-encryption-cli --encrypt `
5                             --input Hello.txt `
6                             --master-keys key=$CmkArn `
7                             --metadata-output $home\Metadata.txt `
8                             --encryption-context purpose=test `
9                             --output .
```

When the encrypt command succeeds, it does not return any output. To determine whether the command succeeded, check the Boolean value in the $? variable. When the command succeeds, the value of $? is 0 (Bash) or `True` (PowerShell). When the command fails, the value of $? is non-zero (Bash) or `False` (PowerShell).

[Bash]

```
1 $ echo $?
2 0
```

[PowerShell]

```
1 PS C:\> $?
2 True
```

You can also use a directory listing command to see that the encrypt command created a new file, `hello.txt`.`encrypted`. Because the encrypt command did not specify a file name for the output, the AWS Encryption CLI wrote the output to a file with the same name as the input file plus a `.encrypted` suffix. To use a different suffix, or suppress the suffix, use the `--suffix` parameter.

The `hello.txt.encrypted` file contains an encrypted message that includes the ciphertext of the `hello.txt` file, an encrypted copy of the data key, and additional metadata, including the encryption context.

[Bash]

```
1 $ ls
2 hello.txt  hello.txt.encrypted
```

[PowerShell]

```
1 PS C:\> dir
2
3     Directory: C:\TestCLI
4
```

```
5 Mode              LastWriteTime         Length Name
6 ----              -------------         ------ ----
7 -a----    9/15/2017   5:57 PM               11 Hello.txt
8 -a----    9/17/2017   1:06 PM              585 Hello.txt.encrypted
```

Decrypting a File

This example uses the AWS Encryption CLI to decrypt the contents of the `Hello.txt.encrypted` file that was encrypted in the previous example.

The decrypt command uses the `--decrypt` parameter to indicate the operation and `--input` parameter to identify the file to decrypt. The value of the `--output` parameter is a dot that represents the current directory.

This command does not have a `--master-keys` parameter. A `--master-keys` parameter is required in decrypt commands only when you are using a custom master key provider. If you are using an AWS KMS CMK, you cannot specify a master key, because AWS KMS derives it from the encrypted message.

The `--encryption-context` parameter is optional in the decrypt command, even when an encryption context is provided in the encrypt command. In this case, the decrypt command uses the same encryption context that was provided in the encrypt command. Before decrypting, the AWS Encryption CLI verifies that the encryption context in the encrypted message includes a `purpose=test` pair. If it does not, the decrypt command fails.

The `--metadata-output` parameter specifies a file for metadata about the decryption operation. The value of the `--output` parameter, a dot (.), writes the output file to the current directory.

[Bash]

```
1 $ aws-encryption-cli --decrypt \
2                       --input hello.txt.encrypted \
3                       --encryption-context purpose=test \
4                       --metadata-output ~/metadata \
5                       --output .
```

[PowerShell]

```
1 PS C:\> aws-encryption-cli --decrypt `
2                       --input Hello.txt.encrypted `
3                       --encryption-context purpose=test `
4                       --metadata-output $home\Metadata.txt `
5                       --output .
```

When a decrypt command succeeds, it does not return any output. To determine whether the command succeeded, get the value of the $? variable. You can also use a directory listing command to see that the command created a new file with a `.decrypted` suffix. To see the plaintext content, use a command to get the file content, such as `cat` or Get-Content.

```
1 $ ls
2 hello.txt   hello.txt.encrypted   hello.txt.encrypted.decrypted
3
4 $ cat hello.txt.encrypted.decrypted
5 Hello World
```

[PowerShell]

```
1 PS C:\> dir
2
3    Directory: C:\TestCLI
4
5 Mode                LastWriteTime         Length Name
6 ----                -------------         ------ ----
7 -a----         9/17/2017   1:01 PM             11 Hello.txt
8 -a----         9/17/2017   1:06 PM            585 Hello.txt.encrypted
9 -a----         9/17/2017   1:08 PM             11 Hello.txt.encrypted.decrypted
10
11
12 PS C:\> Get-Content Hello.txt.encrypted.decrypted
13 Hello World
```

Encrypting All Files in a Directory

This example uses the AWS Encryption CLI to encrypt the contents of all of the files in a directory.

When a command affects multiple files, the AWS Encryption CLI processes each file individually. It gets the file contents, gets a unique data key for the file from the master key, encrypts the file contents under the data key, and writes the results to a new file in the output directory. As a result, you can decrypt the output files independently.

This listing of the TestDir directory shows the plaintext files that we want to encrypt.

[Bash]

```
1 $ ls testdir
2 cool-new-thing.py   hello.txt   employees.csv
```

[PowerShell]

```
1 PS C:\> dir C:\TestDir
2
3    Directory: C:\TestDir
4
5 Mode                LastWriteTime         Length Name
```

49

```
6  ----                 -------------              ------ ----
7  -a----     9/12/2017   3:11 PM            2139 cool-new-thing.py
8  -a----     9/15/2017   5:57 PM              11 Hello.txt
9  -a----     9/17/2017   1:44 PM              46 Employees.csv
```

The first command saves the Amazon Resource Name (ARN) of an AWS KMS customer master key (CMK) in the $cmkArn variable.

The second command encrypts the content of files in the TestDir directory and writes the files of encrypted content to the TestEnc directory. If the TestEnc directory doesn't exist, the command fails. Because the input location is a directory, the --recursive parameter is required.

The --master-keys parameter, and its required **key** attribute, specify the master key. The encrypt command includes an encryption context, dept=IT. When you specify an encryption context in a command that encrypts multiple files, the same encryption context is used for all of the files.

The command also has a --metadata-output parameter to tell the AWS Encryption CLI where to write the metadata about the encryption operations. The AWS Encryption CLI writes one metadata record for each file that was encrypted.

When the command completes, the AWS Encryption CLI writes the encrypted files to the TestEnc directory, but it does not return any output.

The final command lists the files in the TestEnc directory. There is one output file of encrypted content for each input file of plaintext content. Because the command did not specify an alternate suffix, the encrypt command appended .encrypted to each of the input file names.

[**Bash**]

```
1  # To run this example, replace the fictitious CMK ARN with a valid master key identifier.
2  $  cmkArn=arn:aws:kms:us-west-2:111122223333:key/1234abcd-12ab-34cd-56ef-1234567890ab
3
4  $ aws-encryption-cli --encrypt \
5                    --input testdir --recursive\
6                    --master-keys key=$cmkArn \
7                    --encryption-context dept=IT \
8                    --metadata-output ~/metadata \
9                    --output testenc
10
11 $ ls testenc
12 cool-new-thing.py.encrypted  employees.csv.encrypted  hello.txt.encrypted
```

[**PowerShell**]

```
1  # To run this example, replace the fictitious CMK ARN with a valid master key identifier.
2  PS C:\> $cmkArn = arn:aws:kms:us-west-2:111122223333:key/1234abcd-12ab-34cd-56ef-1234567890ab
3
4  PS C:\> aws-encryption-cli --encrypt `
5                      --input .\TestDir --recursive `
6                      --master-keys key=$cmkArn `
7                      --encryption-context dept=IT `
8                      --metadata-output .\Metadata\Metadata.txt `
```

```
  9                          --output .\TestEnc
 10
 11 PS C:\> dir .\TestEnc
 12
 13     Directory: C:\TestEnc
 14
 15 Mode                LastWriteTime         Length Name
 16 ----                -------------         ------ ----
 17 -a----         9/17/2017   2:32 PM         2713 cool-new-thing.py.encrypted
 18 -a----         9/17/2017   2:32 PM          620 Hello.txt.encrypted
 19 -a----         9/17/2017   2:32 PM          585 Employees.csv.encrypted
```

Decrypting All Files in a Directory

This example decrypts all files in a directory. It starts with the files in the `TestEnc` directory that were encrypted in the previous example.

[Bash]

```
 1 $ ls testenc
 2 cool-new-thing.py.encrypted  hello.txt.encrypted  employees.csv.encrypted
```

[PowerShell]

```
 1 PS C:\> dir C:\TestEnc
 2
 3     Directory: C:\TestEnc
 4
 5 Mode                LastWriteTime         Length Name
 6 ----                -------------         ------ ----
 7 -a----         9/17/2017   2:32 PM         2713 cool-new-thing.py.encrypted
 8 -a----         9/17/2017   2:32 PM          620 Hello.txt.encrypted
 9 -a----         9/17/2017   2:32 PM          585 Employees.csv.encrypted
```

This decrypt command decrypts all of the files in the TestEnc directory and writes the plaintext files to the TestDec directory. Because the encrypted files were encrypted under an AWS KMS CMK, there is no `--master-keys` parameter in the command. The command uses the `--interactive` parameter to tell the AWS Encryption CLI to prompt you before overwriting a file with the same name.

This command also uses the encryption context that was provided when the files were encrypted. When decrypting multiple files, the AWS Encryption CLI checks the encryption context of every file. If the encryption context check on any file fails, the AWS Encryption CLI rejects the file, writes a warning, records the failure in the metadata, and then continues checking the remaining files. If the AWS Encryption CLI fails to decrypt a file for any other reason, the entire decrypt command fails immediately.

In this example, the encrypted messages in all of the input files contain the `dept=IT` encryption context element. However, if you were decrypting messages with different encryption contexts, you might still be able to verify part of the encryption context. For example, if some messages had an encryption context of `dept=finance` and others had `dept=IT`, you could verify that the encryption context always contains a `dept` name without specifying the value. If you wanted to be more specific, you could decrypt the files in separate commands.

The decrypt command does not return any output, but you can use a directory listing command to see that it created new files with the `.decrypted` suffix. To see the plaintext content, use a command to get the file content.

[**Bash**]

```
1 $ aws-encryption-cli --decrypt --input testenc --recursive \
2                      --encryption-context dept=IT \
3                      --metadata-output ~/metadata \
4                      --output testdec --interactive
5
6 $ ls testdec
7 cool-new-thing.py.encrypted.decrypted   hello.txt.encrypted.decrypted   employees.csv.encrypted.
    decrypted
```

[**PowerShell**]

```
1 PS C:\> aws-encryption-cli --decrypt `
2                      --input C:\TestEnc --recursive `
3                      --encryption-context dept=IT `
4                      --metadata-output $home\Metadata.txt `
5                      --output C:\TestDec --interactive
6
7 PS C:\> dir .\TestDec
8
9
10    Mode                LastWriteTime         Length Name
11    ----                -------------         ------ ----
12    -a----        10/8/2017   4:57 PM           2139 cool-new-thing.py.encrypted.decrypted
13    -a----        10/8/2017   4:57 PM             46 Employees.csv.encrypted.decrypted
14    -a----        10/8/2017   4:57 PM             11 Hello.txt.encrypted.decrypted
```

Encrypting and Decrypting on the Command Line

These examples show you how to pipe input to commands (stdin) and write output to the command line (stdout). They explain how to represent stdin and stdout in a command and how to use the built-in Base64 encoding tools to prevent the shell from misinterpreting non-ASCII characters.

This example pipes a plaintext string to an encrypt command and saves the encrypted message in a variable. Then, it pipes the encrypted message in the variable to a decrypt command, which writes its output to the pipeline (stdout).

The example consists of three commands:

- The first command saves the Amazon Resource Name (ARN) of an AWS KMS customer master key (CMK) in the `$cmkArn` variable.

```
1 $ cmkArn=arn:aws:kms:us-west-2:111122223333:key/1234abcd-12ab-34cd-56ef-1234567890ab
```

```
1 PS C:\> $cmkArn = arn:aws:kms:us-west-2:111122223333:key/1234abcd-12ab-34cd-56ef-1234567890ab
```

- The second command pipes the `Hello World` string to the encrypt command and saves the result in the `$encrypted` variable.

  The `--input` and `--output` parameters are required in all AWS Encryption CLI commands. To indicate that input is being piped to the command (stdin), use a hyphen (-) for the value of the `--input` parameter. To send the output to the command line (stdout), use a hyphen for the value of the `--output` parameter.

  The `--encode` parameter Base64-encodes the output before returning it. This prevents the shell from misinterpreting the non-ASCII characters in the encrypted message.

  Because this command is just a proof of concept, we omit the encryption context and suppress the metadata (`-S`).

```
1 $ encrypted=$(echo 'Hello World' | aws-encryption-cli --encrypt -S \
2                                     --input - --output - --encode \
3                                     --master-keys key=$cmkArn )
```

```
1 PS C:\> $encrypted = 'Hello World' | aws-encryption-cli --encrypt -S `
2                                      --input - --output - --encode `
3                                      --master-keys key=$cmkArn
```

- The third command pipes the encrypted message in the `$encrypted` variable to the decrypt command.

  This decrypt command uses `--input -` to indicate that input is coming from the pipeline (stdin) and `--output -` to send the output to the pipeline (stdout). (The input parameter takes the location of the input, not the actual input bytes, so you cannot use the `$encrypted` variable as the value of the `--input` parameter.)

  Because the output was encrypted and then encoded, the decrypt command uses the `--decode` parameter to decode Base64-encoded input before decrypting it. You can also use the `--decode` parameter to decode Base64-encoded input before encrypting it.

  Again, the command omits the encryption context and suppresses the metadata (`-S`).

```
1 $ echo $encrypted | aws-encryption-cli --decrypt --input - --output - --decode -S
2 Hello World
```

```
1 PS C:\> $encrypted | aws-encryption-cli --decrypt --input - --output - --decode -S
2 Hello World
```

You can also perform the encrypt and decrypt operations in a single command without the intervening variable.

As in the previous example, the --input and --output parameters have a - value and the command uses the --encode parameter to encode the output and the --decode parameter to decode the input.

```
1 $ cmkArn=arn:aws:kms:us-west-2:111122223333:key/1234abcd-12ab-34cd-56ef-1234567890ab
2
3 $ echo 'Hello World' |
4        aws-encryption-cli --encrypt --master-keys key=$cmkArn --input - --output - --encode -
            S |
5        aws-encryption-cli --decrypt  --input - --output - --decode -S
6 Hello World
```

```
1 PS C:\> $cmkArn = arn:aws:kms:us-west-2:111122223333:key/1234abcd-12ab-34cd-56ef-1234567890ab
2
3 PS C:\> 'Hello World' |
4            aws-encryption-cli --encrypt --master-keys key=$cmkArn --input - --output - --
                encode -S |
5            aws-encryption-cli --decrypt --input - --output - --decode -S
6 Hello World
```

Using Multiple Master Keys

This example shows how to use multiple master keys when encrypting and decrypting data in the AWS Encryption CLI.

When you use multiple master keys to encrypt data, any one of the master keys can be used to decrypt the data. This strategy assures that you can decrypt the data even if one of the master keys is unavailable. If you are storing the encrypted data in multiple AWS Regions, this strategy lets you use a master key in the same Region to decrypt the data.

When you encrypt with multiple master keys, the first master key plays a special role. It generates the data key that is used to encrypt the data. The remaining master keys encrypt the plaintext data key. The resulting encrypted message includes the encrypted data and a collection of encrypted data keys, one for each master key. Although the first master key generated the data key, any of the master keys can decrypt one of the data keys, which can be used to decrypt the data.

Encrypting with Three Master Keys

This example command uses three master keys to encrypt the `Finance.log` file, one in each of three AWS Regions.

It writes the encrypted message to the `Archive` directory. The command uses the `--suffix` parameter with no value to suppress the suffix, so the input and output files names will be the same.

The command uses the `--master-keys` parameter with three **key** attributes. You can also use multiple `--master-keys` parameters in the same command.

To encrypt the log file, the AWS Encryption CLI asks the first master key in the list, `$cmk1`, to generate the data key that it uses to encrypt the data. Then, it uses each of the other master keys to encrypt the plaintext copy of the data key. The encrypted message in the output file includes all three of the encrypted data keys.

[**Bash**]

```
1 $ cmk1=arn:aws:kms:us-west-2:111122223333:key/1234abcd-12ab-34cd-56ef-1234567890ab
2 $ cmk2=arn:aws:kms:us-east-2:111122223333:key/0987ab65-43cd-21ef-09ab-87654321cdef
3 $ cmk3=arn:aws:kms:ap-southeast-1:111122223333:key/1a2b3c4d-5e6f-1a2b-3c4d-5e6f1a2b3c4d
4
5 $ aws-encryption-cli --encrypt --input /logs/finance.log \
6                              --output /archive --suffix \
7                              --encryption-context class=log \
8                              --metadata-output ~/metadata \
9                              --master-keys key=$cmk1 key=$cmk2 key=$cmk3
```

[**PowerShell**]

```
1 PS C:\> $cmk1 = arn:aws:kms:us-west-2:111122223333:key/1234abcd-12ab-34cd-56ef-1234567890ab
2 PS C:\> $cmk2 = arn:aws:kms:us-east-2:111122223333:key/0987ab65-43cd-21ef-09ab-87654321cdef
3 PS C:\> $cmk3 = arn:aws:kms:ap-southeast-1:111122223333:key/1a2b3c4d-5e6f-1a2b-3c4d-5e6f1a2b3c4d
4
5 PS C:\> aws-encryption-cli --encrypt --input D:\Logs\Finance.log `
6                              --output D:\Archive --suffix `
7                              --encryption-context class=log `
8                              --metadata-output $home\Metadata.txt `
9                              --master-keys key=$cmk1 key=$cmk2 key=$cmk3
```

This command decrypts the encrypted copy of the `Finance.log` file and writes it to a `Finance.log.clear` file in the `Finance` directory.

When you decrypt data that was encrypted under AWS KMS CMKs, you cannot tell AWS KMS to use a particular CMK to decrypt the data. The **key** attribute of the `--master-keys` parameter is not valid in a decrypt command with the **aws-kms** provider. The AWS Encryption CLI can use any of the CMKs that were used to encrypt the data, provided that the AWS credentials you are using have permission to call the Decrypt API on the master key. For more information, see Authentication and Access Control for AWS KMS.

```
1 $ aws-encryption-cli --decrypt --input /archive/finance.log \
2                      --output /finance --suffix '.clear' \
3                      --metadata-output ~/metadata \
4                      --encryption-context class=log
```

```
1 PS C:\> aws-encryption-cli --decrypt `
2                        --input D:\Archive\Finance.log `
3                        --output D:\Finance --suffix '.clear' `
4                        --metadata-output .\Metadata\Metadata.txt `
5                        --encryption-context class=log
```

Encrypting and Decrypting in Scripts

This example shows how to use the AWS Encryption CLI in scripts. You can write scripts that just encrypt and decrypt data, or scripts that encrypt or decrypt as part of a data management process.

In this example, the script gets a collection of log files, compresses them, encrypts them, and then copies the encrypted files to an Amazon S3 bucket. This script processes each file separately, so that you can decrypt and expand them independently.

When you compress and encrypt files, be sure to compress before you encrypt. Properly encrypted data is not compressible.

Warning
Be careful when compressing data that includes both secrets and data that might be controlled by a malicious actor. The final size of the compressed data might inadvertently reveal sensitive information about its contents.

You can find the complete scripts in the Examples directory of the aws-encryption-sdk-cli repository in GitHub.

```
1 #Requires -Modules AWSPowerShell, Microsoft.PowerShell.Archive
2 Param
3 (
4     [Parameter(Mandatory)]
5     [ValidateScript({Test-Path $_})]
6     [String[]]
7     $FilePath,
8
9     [Parameter()]
10    [Switch]
11    $Recurse,
12
13    [Parameter(Mandatory=$true)]
14    [String]
15    $masterKeyID,
16
```

```powershell
17        [Parameter()]
18        [String]
19        $masterKeyProvider = 'aws-kms',
20
21        [Parameter(Mandatory)]
22        [ValidateScript({Test-Path $_})]
23        [String]
24        $ZipDirectory,
25
26        [Parameter(Mandatory)]
27        [ValidateScript({Test-Path $_})]
28        [String]
29        $EncryptDirectory,
30
31        [Parameter()]
32        [String]
33        $EncryptionContext,
34
35        [Parameter(Mandatory)]
36        [ValidateScript({Test-Path $_})]
37        [String]
38        $MetadataDirectory,
39
40        [Parameter(Mandatory)]
41        [ValidateScript({Test-S3Bucket -BucketName $_})]
42        [String]
43        $S3Bucket,
44
45        [Parameter()]
46        [String]
47        $S3BucketFolder
48 )
49
50 BEGIN {}
51 PROCESS {
52     if ($files = dir $FilePath -Recurse:$Recurse)
53     {
54
55         # Step 1: Compress
56         foreach ($file in $files)
57         {
58             $fileName = $file.Name
59             try
60             {
61                 Microsoft.PowerShell.Archive\Compress-Archive -Path $file.FullName -
                     DestinationPath $ZipDirectory\$filename.zip
62             }
63             catch
64             {
65                 Write-Error "Zip failed on $file.FullName"
66             }
67
68             # Step 2: Encrypt
69             if (-not (Test-Path "$ZipDirectory\$filename.zip"))
```

```
 70                    {
 71                            Write-Error "Cannot find zipped file: $ZipDirectory\$filename.zip"
 72                    }
 73                else
 74                    {
 75                        # 2>&1 captures command output
 76                        $err = (aws-encryption-cli -e -i "$ZipDirectory\$filename.zip" `
 77                                                    -o $EncryptDirectory `
 78                                                    -m key=$masterKeyID provider=$masterKeyProvider `
 79                                                    -c $EncryptionContext `
 80                                                    --metadata-output $MetadataDirectory `
 81                                                    -v) 2>&1
 82
 83                        # Check error status
 84                        if ($? -eq $false)
 85                        {
 86                            # Write the error
 87                            $err
 88                        }
 89                        elseif (Test-Path "$EncryptDirectory\$fileName.zip.encrypted")
 90                        {
 91                            # Step 3: Write to S3 bucket
 92                            if ($S3BucketFolder)
 93                            {
 94                                Write-S3Object -BucketName $S3Bucket -File "$EncryptDirectory\$fileName.
                                        zip.encrypted" -Key "$S3BucketFolder/$fileName.zip.encrypted"
 95
 96                            }
 97                            else
 98                            {
 99                                Write-S3Object -BucketName $S3Bucket -File "$EncryptDirectory\$fileName.
                                        zip.encrypted"
100                            }
101                        }
102                    }
103                }
104            }
105 }
```

Using Data Key Caching

This example uses data key caching in a command that encrypts a large number of files.

By default, the AWS Encryption CLI (and other versions of the AWS Encryption SDK) generates a unique data key for each file that it encrypts. Although using a unique data key for each operation is a cryptographic best practice, limited reuse of data keys is acceptable for some situations. If you are considering data key caching, consult with a security engineer to understand the security requirements of your application and determine security thresholds that are right for you.

In this example, data key caching speeds up the encryption operation by reducing the frequency of requests to the master key provider.

The command in this example encrypts a large directory with multiple subdirectories that contain a total of approximately 800 small log files. The first command saves the ARN of the CMK in a `cmkARN` variable. The second command encrypts all of the files in the input directory (recursively) and writes them to an archive directory. The command uses the `--suffix` parameter to specify the `.archive` suffix.

The `--caching` parameter enables data key caching. The **capacity** attribute, which limits the number of data keys in the cache, is set to 1, because serial file processing never uses more than one data key at a time. The **max_age** attribute, which determines how long the cached data key can used, is set to 10 seconds.

The optional **max_messages_encrypted** attribute is set to 10 messages, so a single data key is never used to encrypt more than 10 files. Limiting the number of files encrypted by each data key reduces the number of files that would be affected in the unlikely event that a data key was compromised.

To run this command on log files that your operating system generates, you might need administrator permissions (`sudo` in Linux; **Run as Administrator** in Windows).

[**Bash**]

```
1 $ cmkArn=arn:aws:kms:us-west-2:111122223333:key/1234abcd-12ab-34cd-56ef-1234567890ab
2
3 $ aws-encryption-cli --encrypt \
4                        --input /var/log/httpd --recursive \
5                        --output ~/archive --suffix .archive \
6                        --master-keys key=$cmkArn \
7                        --encryption-context class=log \
8                        --suppress-metadata \
9                        --caching capacity=1 max_age=10 max_messages_encrypted=10
```

[**PowerShell**]

```
1 PS C:\> $cmkArn = arn:aws:kms:us-west-2:111122223333:key/1234abcd-12ab-34cd-56ef-1234567890ab
2
3 PS C:\> aws-encryption-cli --encrypt `
4                        --input C:\Windows\Logs --recursive `
5                        --output $home\Archive --suffix '.archive' `
6                        --master-keys key=$cmkARN `
7                        --encryption-context class=log `
8                        --suppress-metadata `
9                        --caching capacity=1 max_age=10 max_messages_encrypted=10
```

To test the effect of data key caching, this example uses the Measure-Command cmdlet in PowerShell. When you run this example without data key caching, it takes about 25 seconds to complete. This process generates a new data key for each file in the directory.

```
1 PS C:\> Measure-Command {aws-encryption-cli --encrypt `
2                                --input C:\Windows\Logs --recursive `
3                                --output $home\Archive  --suffix '.archive' `
4                                --master-keys key=$cmkARN `
5                                --encryption-context class=log `
6                                --suppress-metadata }
7
8
```

```
 9 Days            : 0
10 Hours           : 0
11 Minutes         : 0
12 Seconds         : 25
13 Milliseconds    : 453
14 Ticks           : 254531202
15 TotalDays       : 0.000294596298611111
16 TotalHours      : 0.00707031116666667
17 TotalMinutes    : 0.42421867
18 TotalSeconds    : 25.4531202
19 TotalMilliseconds : 25453.1202
```

Data key caching makes the process quicker, even when you limit each data key to a maximum of 10 files. The command now takes less than 12 seconds to complete and reduces the number of calls to the master key provider to 1/10 of the original value.

```
 1 PS C:\> Measure-Command {aws-encryption-cli --encrypt `
 2                                     --input C:\Windows\Logs --recursive `
 3                                     --output $home\Archive  --suffix '.archive' `
 4                                     --master-keys key=$cmkARN `
 5                                     --encryption-context class=log `
 6                                     --suppress-metadata `
 7                                     --caching capacity=1 max_age=10
                                           max_messages_encrypted=10}
 8
 9
10 Days            : 0
11 Hours           : 0
12 Minutes         : 0
13 Seconds         : 11
14 Milliseconds    : 813
15 Ticks           : 118132640
16 TotalDays       : 0.000136727592592593
17 TotalHours      : 0.00328146222222222
18 TotalMinutes    : 0.196887733333333
19 TotalSeconds    : 11.813264
20 TotalMilliseconds : 11813.264
```

If you eliminate the `max_messages_encrypted` restriction, all files are encrypted under the same data key. This change increases the risk of reusing data keys without making the process much faster. However, it reduces the number of calls to the master key provider to 1.

```
 1 PS C:\> Measure-Command {aws-encryption-cli --encrypt `
 2                                     --input C:\Windows\Logs --recursive `
 3                                     --output $home\Archive  --suffix '.archive' `
 4                                     --master-keys key=$cmkARN `
 5                                     --encryption-context class=log `
 6                                     --suppress-metadata `
 7                                     --caching capacity=1 max_age=10}
 8
 9
10 Days            : 0
11 Hours           : 0
12 Minutes         : 0
13 Seconds         : 10
14 Milliseconds    : 252
```

```
15 Ticks              : 102523367
16 TotalDays          : 0.000118661304398148
17 TotalHours         : 0.00284787130555556
18 TotalMinutes       : 0.170872278333333
19 TotalSeconds       : 10.2523367
20 TotalMilliseconds : 10252.3367
```

AWS Encryption SDK CLI Syntax and Parameter Reference

This topic provides syntax diagrams and brief parameter descriptions to help you use the AWS Encryption SDK Command Line Interface (CLI). For help with master keys and other parameters, see How to Use the AWS Encryption SDK Command Line Interface. For example, see Examples of the AWS Encryption SDK Command Line Interface. For complete documentation, see Read the Docs.

Topics

- AWS Encryption CLI Syntax
- AWS Encryption CLI Command Line Parameters
- Advanced Parameters

AWS Encryption CLI Syntax

These AWS Encryption CLI syntax diagrams show the syntax for each task that you perform with the AWS Encryption CLI.

Get Help
To get the full AWS Encryption CLI syntax with parameter descriptions, use --help or -h.

```
1 aws-encryption-cli (--help | -h)
```

Get the Version
To get the version number of your AWS Encryption CLI installation, use --version. Be sure to include the version when you ask questions, report problems, or share tips about using the AWS Encryption CLI.

```
1 aws-encryption-cli --version
```

Encrypt Data
The following syntax diagram shows the parameters that an encrypt command uses.

```
1 aws-encryption-cli --encrypt
2                     --input <input> [--recursive] [--decode]
3                     --output <output> [--interactive] [--no-overwrite] [--suffix [<suffix>]] [--
                          encode]
4                     --master-keys  [--master-keys ...]
5                        key=<keyID> [provider=<provider-name>] [region=<aws-region>] [profile=<
                          aws-profile>]
6                     --metadata-output <location> [--overwrite-metadata] | --suppress-metadata
7                     [--encryption-context <encryption_context> [<encryption_context> ...]]
8                     [--algorithm <algorithm_suite>]
9                     [--caching <attributes>]
10                    [--frame-length <length>]
11                    [-v | -vv | -vvv | -vvvv]
12                    [--quiet]
```

Decrypt Data
The following syntax diagram shows the parameters that a decrypt command uses.

```
1 aws-encryption-cli --decrypt
2                     --input <input> [--recursive] [--decode]
3                     --output <output> [--interactive] [--no-overwrite]  [--suffix [<suffix>]] [--
                          encode]
4                     --metadata-output <location> [--overwrite-metadata] | --suppress-metadata
5                     [--master-keys [--master-keys ...]
```

```
6            [key=<keyID>] [provider=<provider-name>] [region=<aws-region>] [profile=<
                aws-profile>]]
7        [--encryption-context <encryption_context> [<encryption_context> ...]]
8        [--caching <attributes>]
9        [--max-length <length>]
10       [-v | -vv | -vvv | -vvvv]
11       [--quiet]
```

Use Configuration Files

You can refer to configuration files that contain parameters and their values. This is equivalent to typing the parameters and values in the command. For an example, see How to Store Parameters in a Configuration File.

```
1 aws-encryption-cli @<configuration_file>
2
3 # In a PowerShell console, use a backtick to escape the @.
4 aws-encryption-cli `@<configuration_file>
```


AWS Encryption CLI Command Line Parameters

This list provides a basic description of the AWS Encryption CLI command parameters. For a complete description, see the aws-encryption-sdk-cli documentation.

--encrypt (-e)
Encrypts the input data. Every command must have an --encrypt or --decrypt parameter.

--decrypt (-d)
Decrypts the input data. Every command must have an --encrypt or --decrypt parameter.

--master-keys (-m)
Specifies the master keys used in encryption and decryption operations. You can use multiple master keys parameters in each command.
The --master-keys parameter is required in encrypt commands. It is required in decrypt commands only when you are using a custom master key provider.
Attributes: The value of the --master-keys parameter consists of the following attributes. The format is attribute_name=value.
key
Identifies the master key. The format is a **key**=ID pair.
The **key** attribute is required in all encrypt commands. When you use an AWS KMS customer master key (CMK) in an encrypt command, the value of the **key** attribute can be a CMK ID or Amazon Resource Name (ARN), an alias, or an alias ARN.
The key attribute is required in decrypt commands when the master key provider is not AWS KMS. The **key** attribute is not permitted in commands that decrypt data that was encrypted under an AWS KMS CMK.
You can specify multiple **key** attributes in each --master-keys parameter value. However, any **provider**, **region**, and **profile** attributes apply to all master keys in the parameter value. To specify master keys with different attribute values, use multiple --master-keys parameters in the command.
provider
Identifies the master key provider. The format is a **provider**=ID pair. The default value, **aws-kms**, represents AWS KMS. This attribute is required only when the master key provider is not AWS KMS.
region
Identifies the AWS Region of an AWS KMS CMK. This attribute is valid only for AWS KMS CMKs. It is used only when the **key** identifier does not specify a region; otherwise, it is ignored. When it is used, it overrides the default region in the AWS CLI named profile.
profile
Identifies an AWS CLI named profile. This attribute is valid only for AWS KMS CMKs. The region in the profile is used only when the key identifier does not specify a region and there is no **region** attribute in the command.

--input (-i)

Specifies the location of the data to encrypt or decrypt. This parameter is required. The value can be a path to a file or directory, or a file name pattern. If you are piping input to the command (stdin), use -.

If the input does not exist, the command completes successfully without error or warning.

--recursive (-r, -R)

Performs the operation on files in the input directory and its subdirectories. This parameter is required when the value of --input is a directory.

--decode

Decodes Base64-encoded input.

If you are decrypting a message that was encrypted and then encoded, you must decode the message before decrypting it. This parameter does that for you.

For example, if you used the --encode parameter in an encrypt command, use the --decode parameter in the corresponding decrypt command. You can also use this parameter to decode Base64-encoded input before you encrypt it.

--output (-o)

Specifies a destination for the output. This parameter is required. The value can be a file name, an existing directory, or -, which writes output to the command line (stdout).

If the specified output directory does not exist, the command fails. If the input contains subdirectories, the AWS Encryption CLI reproduces the subdirectories under the output directory that you specify.

By default, the AWS Encryption CLI overwrites files with the same name. To change that behavior, use the --interactive or --no-overwrite parameters. To suppress the overwrite warning, use the --quiet parameter. If a command that would overwrite an output file fails, the output file is deleted.

--interactive

Prompts before overwriting the file.

--no-overwrite

Does not overwrite files. Instead, if the output file exists, the AWS Encryption CLI skips the corresponding input.

--suffix

Specifies a custom file name suffix for files that the AWS Encryption CLI creates. To indicate no suffix, use the parameter with no value (--suffix).

By default, when the --output parameter does not specify a file name, the output file name has the same name as the input file name plus the suffix. The suffix for encrypt commands is .encrypted. The suffix for decrypt commands is .decrypted.

--encode

Applies Base64 (binary to text) encoding to the output. Encoding prevents the shell host program from misinterpreting non-ASCII characters in output text.

Use this parameter when writing encrypted output to stdout (--output -), especially in a PowerShell console, even when you are piping the output to another command or saving it in a variable.

--metadata-output

Specifies a location for metadata about the cryptographic operations. Enter a path and file name. If the directory does not exist, the command fails. To write the metadata to the command line (stdout), use -.

You cannot write command output (--output) and metadata output (--metadata-output) to stdout in the same command. Also, when the value of --input or --output is a directory (without file names), you cannot write the metadata output to the same directory or to any subdirectory of that directory.

If you specify an existing file, by default, the AWS Encryption CLI appends new metadata records to any content in the file. This feature lets you create a single file that contains the metadata for all of your cryptographic operations. To overwrite the content in an existing file, use the --overwrite-metadata parameter.

The AWS Encryption CLI returns a JSON-formatted metadata record for each encryption or decryption operation that the command performs. Each metadata record includes the full paths to the input and output file, the encryption context, the algorithm suite, and other valuable information that you can use to review the operation and verify that it meets your security standards.

--overwrite-metadata

Overwrites the content in the metadata output file. By default, the --metadata-output parameter appends metadata to any existing content in the file.

--suppress-metadata (-S)
Suppresses the metadata about the encryption or decryption operation.

--encryption-context (-c)
Specifies an encryption context for the operation. This parameter is not required, but it is recommended.

- In an `--encrypt` command, enter one or more `name=value` pairs. Use spaces to separate the pairs.
- In a decrypt command, enter `name=value` pairs, `name` elements with no values, or both. If the `name` or `value` in a `name=value` pair includes spaces or special characters, enclose the entire pair in quotation marks. For example, `--encryption-context "department=software development"`.

--help (-h)
Prints usage and syntax at the command line.

--version
Gets the version of the AWS Encryption CLI.

-v | -vv | -vvv | -vvvv
Displays verbose information, warning, and debugging messages. The detail in the output increases with the number of vs in the parameter. The most detailed setting (-vvvv) returns debugging-level data from the AWS Encryption CLI and all of the components that it uses.

--quiet (-q)
Suppresses warning messages, such as the message that appears when you overwrite an output file.

Advanced Parameters

--algorithm
Specifies an alternate algorithm suite. This parameter is optional and valid only in encrypt commands. By default, the AWS Encryption CLI uses the default algorithm suite for the AWS Encryption SDK, which is AES-GCM with an HKDF, an ECDSA signature, and a 256-bit encryption key. This algorithm suite is recommended for most encryption operations. For a list of alternate values, see Read the Docs.

--frame-length
Creates output with specified frame length. Enter a value in bytes. This parameter is optional and valid only in encrypt commands.

--max-length
Indicates the maximum frame size (or maximum content length for non-framed messages) in bytes to read from encrypted messages. This parameter is optional and valid only in decrypt commands. It is designed to protect you from decrypting extremely large malicious ciphertext.

--caching
Enables the data key caching feature, which reuses data keys, instead of generating a new data key for each input file. This parameter supports an advanced scenario. Be sure to read the Data Key Caching documentation before using this feature.
The `--caching` parameter has the following attributes.
capacity (required)
Determines the maximum number of entries in the cache.
max_age (required)
Determine how long cache entries are used, beginning when they are added to the cache.
max_messages_encrypted
Determines the maximum number of messages that a cached entry can encrypt.
max_bytes_encrypted
Determines the maximum number of bytes that a cached entry can encrypt.

Data Key Caching

Data key caching stores data keys and related cryptographic material in a cache. When you encrypt or decrypt data, the AWS Encryption SDK looks for a matching data key in the cache. If it finds a match, it uses the cached data key rather than generating a new one. Data key caching can improve performance, reduce cost, and help you stay within service limits as your application scales.

Your application can benefit from data key caching if:

- It can reuse data keys.
- It generates numerous data keys.
- Your cryptographic operations are unacceptably slow, expensive, limited, or resource-intensive.

Caching can reduce your use of cryptographic services, such as AWS Key Management Service (AWS KMS). If you are hitting your AWS KMS requests-per-second limit, caching can help. Your application can use cached keys to service some of your data key requests instead of calling AWS KMS. (You can also create a case in the AWS Support Center to raise the limit for your account.)

The AWS Encryption SDK helps you to create and manage your data key cache. It provides a LocalCryptoMaterialsCache and a caching cryptographic materials manager that interacts with the cache and enforces security thresholds that you set. Working together, these components help you to benefit from the efficiency of reusing data keys while maintaining the security of your system.

Data key caching is an optional feature of the AWS Encryption SDK that you should use cautiously. By default, the AWS Encryption SDK generates a new data key for every encryption operation. This technique supports cryptographic best practices, which discourage excessive reuse of data keys. In general, use data key caching only when it is required to meet your performance goals. Then, use the data key caching security thresholds to ensure that you use the minimum amount of caching required to meet your cost and performance goals.

For a detailed discussion of these security tradeoffs, see AWS Encryption SDK: How to Decide if Data Key Caching is Right for Your Application in the AWS Security Blog.

Topics

- How to Implement Data Key Caching
- Setting Cache Security Thresholds
- Data Key Caching Details
- Data Key Caching Example

How to Implement Data Key Caching

This topic shows you how to implement data key caching in your application. It takes you through the process step by step. Then, it combines the steps in a simple example that uses data key caching in an operation to encrypt a string.

Topics

- Implement Data Key Caching: Step-by-Step
- Data Key Caching Example: Encrypt a String

Implement Data Key Caching: Step-by-Step

These step-by-step instructions show you how to create the components that you need to implement data key caching.

- Create a data key cache, such as a LocalCryptoMaterialsCache.

[Java]

```
1 //Cache capacity (maximum number of entries) is required
2 int MAX_CACHE_SIZE = 10;
3
4 CryptoMaterialsCache cache = new LocalCryptoMaterialsCache(MAX_CACHE_SIZE);
```

[Python]

```
1 # Cache capacity (maximum number of entries) is required
2 MAX_CACHE_SIZE = 10
3
4 cache = LocalCryptoMaterialsCache(MAX_CACHE_SIZE)
```

- Create a master key provider. This example uses an AWS Key Management Service (AWS KMS) master key provider.

[Java]

```
1 //Create a KMS master key provider
2 //  The input is the Amazon Resource Name (ARN)
3 //  of a KMS customer master key (CMK)
4
5 MasterKeyProvider<KmsMasterKey> keyProvider = new KmsMasterKeyProvider(kmsCmkArn);
```

67

[Python]

```python
1 # Create a KMS master key provider
2 #   The input is the Amazon Resource Name (ARN)
3 #   of a KMS customer master key (CMK)
4
5 key_provider = aws_encryption_sdk.KMSMasterKeyProvider(key_ids=[kms_cmk_arn])
```

- Create a caching cryptographic materials manager (caching CMM).

  Associate your caching CMM with your cache and master key provider. Then, set cache security thresholds on the caching CMM.

[Java]

```java
1 /*
2  * Security thresholds
3  *    Max entry age is required.
4  *    Max messages (and max bytes) per entry are optional
5  */
6 int MAX_ENTRY_AGE_SECONDS = 60;
7 int MAX_ENTRY_MSGS = 10;
8
9 //Create a caching CMM
10 CryptoMaterialsManager cachingCmm =
11     CachingCryptoMaterialsManager.newBuilder().withMasterKeyProvider(keyProvider)
12                                 .withCache(cache)
13                                 .withMaxAge(MAX_ENTRY_AGE_SECONDS, TimeUnit.SECONDS)
14                                 .withMessageUseLimit(MAX_ENTRY_MSGS)
15     .build();
```

[Python]

```python
1 # Security thresholds
2 #    Max entry age is required.
3 #    Max messages (and max bytes) per entry are optional
4 #
5 MAX_ENTRY_AGE_SECONDS = 60.0
6 MAX_ENTRY_MESSAGES = 10
7
8 # Create a caching CMM
9 caching_cmm = CachingCryptoMaterialsManager(
10     master_key_provider=key_provider,
11     cache=cache,
12     max_age=MAX_ENTRY_AGE_SECONDS,
13     max_messages_encrypted=MAX_ENTRY_MESSAGES
```

That's all you need to do. Then, let the AWS Encryption SDK manage the cache for you, or add your own cache management logic.

When you want to use data key caching in a call to encrypt or decrypt data, specify your caching CMM instead of a master key provider or other CMM.

Note
If you are encrypting data streams, or any data of unknown size, be sure to specify the data size in the request. The AWS Encryption SDK does not use data key caching when encrypting data of unknown size.

[Java]

```
1 // When the call to encryptData specifies a caching CMM,
2 // the encryption operation uses the data key cache
3 //
4 final AwsCrypto encryptionSdk = new AwsCrypto();
5 byte[] message = encryptionSdk.encryptData(cachingCmm, plaintext_source).getResult();
```

[Python]

```
1 # When the call to encrypt specifies a caching CMM,
2 # the encryption operation uses the data key cache
3 #
4 encrypted_message, header = aws_encryption_sdk.encrypt(
5     source=plaintext_source,
6     materials_manager=caching_cmm
7 )
```

Data Key Caching Example: Encrypt a String

This simple code example uses data key caching when encrypting a string. It combines the code from the step-by-step procedure into test code that you can run.

The example creates a LocalCryptoMaterialsCache and a master key provider for an AWS KMS customer master key (CMK). Then, it uses the cache and master key provider to create a caching CMM with appropriate security thresholds. The encryption request specifies the caching CMM, the plaintext data to encrypt, and an encryption context.

To run the example, you need to supply the Amazon Resource Name (ARN) of a KMS CMK. Be sure that you have permission to use the CMK to generate a data key.

For more detailed, real-world examples of creating and using a data key cache, see Data Key Caching Example in Java and Data Key Caching Example in Python.

[**Java**]

```java
1  /*
2   * Copyright 2017 Amazon.com, Inc. or its affiliates. All Rights Reserved.
3   *
4   * Licensed under the Apache License, Version 2.0 (the "License"). You may not use this file
       except
5   * in compliance with the License. A copy of the License is located at
6   *
7   * http://aws.amazon.com/apache2.0
8   *
9   * or in the "license" file accompanying this file. This file is distributed on an "AS IS" BASIS
       ,
10  * WITHOUT WARRANTIES OR CONDITIONS OF ANY KIND, either express or implied. See the License for
       the
11  * specific language governing permissions and limitations under the License.
12  */
13
14
15 import java.nio.charset.StandardCharsets;
16 import java.util.Collections;
17 import java.util.Map;
18 import java.util.concurrent.TimeUnit;
19
20 import javax.xml.bind.DatatypeConverter;
21
22 import com.amazonaws.encryptionsdk.AwsCrypto;
23 import com.amazonaws.encryptionsdk.CryptoMaterialsManager;
24 import com.amazonaws.encryptionsdk.MasterKeyProvider;
25 import com.amazonaws.encryptionsdk.caching.CachingCryptoMaterialsManager;
26 import com.amazonaws.encryptionsdk.caching.CryptoMaterialsCache;
27 import com.amazonaws.encryptionsdk.caching.LocalCryptoMaterialsCache;
28 import com.amazonaws.encryptionsdk.kms.KmsMasterKey;
29 import com.amazonaws.encryptionsdk.kms.KmsMasterKeyProvider;
30
31 /**
32  * <p>
33  * Encrypts a string using an AWS KMS customer master key (CMK) and data key caching
34  *
35  * <p>
36  * Arguments:
37  * <ol>
38  * <li>KMS CMK ARN: To find the Amazon Resource Name of your AWS KMS customer master key (CMK),
39  *     see 'Viewing Keys' at http://docs.aws.amazon.com/kms/latest/developerguide/viewing-keys.
         html
40  * <li>Max entry age: Maximum time (in seconds) that a cached entry can be used
41  * <li>Cache capacity: Maximum number of entries in the cache
42  * </ol>
43  */
44 public class SimpleDataKeyCachingExample {
45     /*
46      * Security thresholds
47      *   Max entry age is required.
48      *   Max messages (and max bytes) per data key are optional
49      */
```

```java
50    private static final int MAX_ENTRY_MSGS = 100;
51
52    public static byte[] encryptWithCaching(String kmsCmkArn, int maxEntryAge, int cacheCapacity
          ) {
53        // Plaintext data to be encrypted
54        byte[] myData = "My plaintext data".getBytes(StandardCharsets.UTF_8);
55
56        // Encryption context
57        final Map<String, String> encryptionContext = Collections.singletonMap("purpose", "test
              ");
58
59        // Create a master key provider
60        MasterKeyProvider<KmsMasterKey> keyProvider = new KmsMasterKeyProvider(kmsCmkArn);
61
62        // Create a cache
63        CryptoMaterialsCache cache = new LocalCryptoMaterialsCache(cacheCapacity);
64
65        // Create a caching CMM
66        CryptoMaterialsManager cachingCmm =
67            CachingCryptoMaterialsManager.newBuilder().withMasterKeyProvider(keyProvider)
68                                    .withCache(cache)
69                                    .withMaxAge(maxEntryAge, TimeUnit.SECONDS)
70                                    .withMessageUseLimit(MAX_ENTRY_MSGS)
71        .build();
72
73        // When the call to encryptData specifies a caching CMM,
74        // the encryption operation uses the data key cache
75        //
76        final AwsCrypto encryptionSdk = new AwsCrypto();
77        return encryptionSdk.encryptData(cachingCmm, myData, encryptionContext).getResult();
78 }
```

[Python]

```python
1  # Copyright 2017 Amazon.com, Inc. or its affiliates. All Rights Reserved.
2  #
3  # Licensed under the Apache License, Version 2.0 (the "License"). You
4  # may not use this file except in compliance with the License. A copy of
5  # the License is located at
6  #
7  # http://aws.amazon.com/apache2.0/
8  #
9  # or in the "license" file accompanying this file. This file is
10 # distributed on an "AS IS" BASIS, WITHOUT WARRANTIES OR CONDITIONS OF
11 # ANY KIND, either express or implied. See the License for the specific
12 # language governing permissions and limitations under the License.
13 """Example of basic configuration and use of data key caching."""
14 import aws_encryption_sdk
15
16
17 def encrypt_with_caching(kms_cmk_arn, max_age_in_cache, cache_capacity):
18     """Encrypts a string using an AWS KMS customer master key (CMK) and data key caching.
19
```

```
20    :param str kms_cmk_arn: Amazon Resource Name (ARN) of the KMS customer master key
21    :param float max_age_in_cache: Maximum time in seconds that a cached entry can be used
22    :param int cache_capacity: Maximum number of entries in the cache
23    """
24    # Data to be encrypted
25    my_data = 'My plaintext data'
26
27    # Security thresholds
28    #   Max messages (and max bytes) per data key are optional
29    MAX_ENTRY_MESSAGES = 100
30
31    # Create an encryption context.
32    encryption_context = {'purpose': 'test'}
33
34    # Create a master key provider for the KMS master key
35    key_provider = aws_encryption_sdk.KMSMasterKeyProvider(key_ids=[kms_cmk_arn])
36
37    # Create a cache
38    cache = aws_encryption_sdk.LocalCryptoMaterialsCache(cache_capacity)
39
40    # Create a caching CMM
41    caching_cmm = aws_encryption_sdk.CachingCryptoMaterialsManager(
42        master_key_provider=key_provider,
43        cache=cache,
44        max_age=max_age_in_cache,
45        max_messages_encrypted=MAX_ENTRY_MESSAGES
46    )
47
48    # When the encrypt request specifies a caching CMM,
49    # the encryption operation uses the data key cache
50    encrypted_message, _header = aws_encryption_sdk.encrypt(
51        source=my_data,
52        materials_manager=caching_cmm,
53        encryption_context=encryption_context
54    )
55
56    return encrypted_message
```

Setting Cache Security Thresholds

When you implement data key caching, you need to configure the security thresholds that the caching CMM enforces.

The security thresholds help you to limit how long each cached data key is used and how much data is protected under each data key. The caching CMM returns cached data keys only when the cache entry conforms to all of the security thresholds. If the cache entry exceeds any threshold, the entry is not used for the current operation and it is evicted from the cache.

As a rule, use the minimum amount of caching that is required to meet your cost and performance goals.

The AWS Encryption SDK only caches data keys that are encrypted by using a key derivation function. Also, it establishes upper limits for the threshold values. These restrictions ensure that data keys are not reused beyond their cryptographic limits. However, because your plaintext data keys are cached (in memory, by default), try to minimize the time that the keys are saved . Also, try to limit the data that might be exposed if a key is compromised.

For examples of setting cache security thresholds, see AWS Encryption SDK: How to Decide if Data Key Caching is Right for Your Application in the AWS Security Blog.

Note
The caching CMM enforces all of the following thresholds. If you do not specify an optional value, the caching CMM uses the default value.
To disable data key caching temporarily, do not set the cache capacity or security thresholds to 0. Instead, use the *null cryptographic materials cache* (NullCryptoMaterialsCache) that the AWS Encryption SDK provides. The NullCryptoMaterialsCache returns a miss for every get request and does not respond to put requests. For more information, see the SDK for your programming language.

Maximum age (required)
Determines how long a cached entry can be used, beginning when it was added. This value is required. Enter a value greater than 0. There is no maximum value.
The LocalCryptoMaterialsCache tries to evict cache entries as soon as possible after they reach the maximum age value. Other conforming caches might perform differently.
Use the shortest interval that still allows your application to benefit from the cache. You can use the maximum age threshold like a key rotation policy. Use it to limit reuse of data keys, minimize exposure of cryptographic materials, and evict data keys whose policies might have changed while they were cached.

Maximum messages encrypted (optional)
Specifies the maximum number of messages that a cached data key can encrypt. This value is optional. Enter a value between 1 and 2^{32} messages. The default value is 2^{32} messages.
Set the number of messages protected by each cached key to be large enough to get value from reuse, but small enough to limit the number of messages that might be exposed if a key is compromised.

Maximum bytes encrypted (optional)
Specifies the maximum number of bytes that a cached data key can encrypt. This value is optional. Enter a value between 0 and $2^{63} - 1$. The default value is $2^{63} - 1$. A value of 0 lets you encrypt empty message strings. The first use of each data key (before caching) is exempt from this threshold. Also, to enforce this threshold, requests to encrypt data of unknown size, such as streamed data with no length specifier, do not use the data key cache.
The bytes in the current request are included when evaluating this threshold. If the bytes processed, plus current bytes, exceed the threshold, the cached data key is evicted from the cache, even though it might have been used on a smaller request.

Data Key Caching Details

Most applications can use the default implementation of data key caching without writing custom code. This section describes the default implementation and some details about options.

Topics

- How Data Key Caching Works
- Creating a Cryptographic Materials Cache
- Creating a Caching Cryptographic Materials Manager
- What Is in a Data Key Cache Entry?
- Encryption Context: How to Select Cache Entries

How Data Key Caching Works

When you use data key caching in a request to encrypt or decrypt data, the AWS Encryption SDK first searches the cache for a data key that matches the request. If it finds a valid match, it uses the cached data key to encrypt the data. Otherwise, it generates a new data key, just as it would without the cache.

In addition to a cache, data key caching uses a caching cryptographic materials manager (caching CMM). The caching CMM is a specialized cryptographic materials manager (CMM) that interacts with a cache and an underlying CMM or master key provider. The caching CMM caches the data keys that its underlying CMM (or master key provider) returns. The caching CMM also enforces cache security thresholds that you set.

To prevent the wrong data key from being selected from the cache, each caching CMM requires that several properties of each cached data key match the materials request, as follows:

- For encryption material requests, the cached entry and the request must have the same algorithm suite, encryption context (even when empty), and partition name (a string that identifies the caching CMM).
- For decryption material requests, the cached entry and the request must have the same algorithm suite, encryption context (even when empty), and partition name (a string that identifies the caching CMM).

Note
The AWS Encryption SDK caches data keys only when the algorithm suite uses a key derivation function. Data key caching is not used for data of unknown size, such as streamed data. This allows the caching CMM to properly enforce the maximum bytes threshold. To avoid this behavior, add the data length to the encryption request.

The following workflows show how a request to encrypt data is processed with and without data key caching. They show how the caching components that you create, including the cache and the caching CMM, are used in the process.

Encrypt Data without Caching

To generate a data key without caching:

1. An application asks the AWS Encryption SDK to encrypt data.

   The request specifies a cryptographic materials manager (CMM) or master key provider. If you specify a master key provider, the AWS Encryption SDK creates a default CMM that interacts with the master key provider you specified.

2. The AWS Encryption SDK asks the CMM for a data key to encrypt the data (get cryptographic materials).

3. The CMM asks its master key provider for master keys (or objects that represent master keys). Then, it uses the master keys to generate a new data key. This might involve a call to a cryptographic service, such as AWS Key Management Service (AWS KMS). The CMM returns plaintext and encrypted copies of the data key to the AWS Encryption SDK.

4. The AWS Encryption SDK uses the plaintext data key to encrypt the data and it returns an encrypted message to the user.

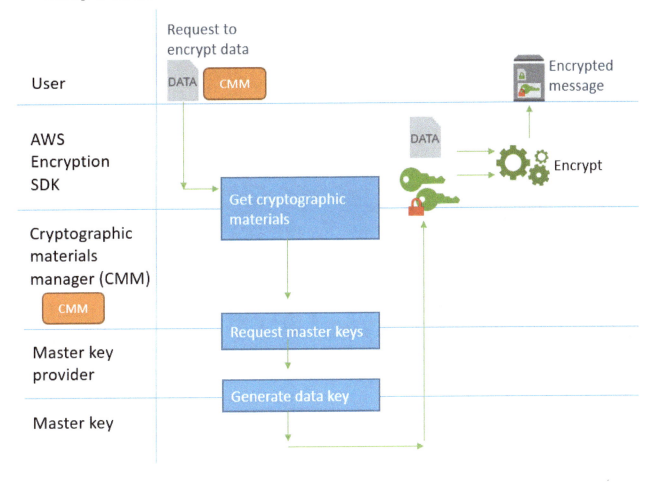

Encrypt Data with Caching

To generate a data key with data key caching:

1. An application asks the AWS Encryption SDK to encrypt data.

   The request specifies a caching cryptographic materials manager (caching CMM) that is associated with a default cryptographic materials manager (CMM) or a master key provider. If you specify a master key provider, the SDK creates a default CMM for you.

2. The SDK asks the specified caching CMM for a data key to encrypt the data (get cryptographic materials).

3. The caching CMM requests a data key from the cache.

   1. If the cache finds a match, it updates the age and use values of the matched cache entry, and returns the cached data key to the caching CMM.

      If the cache entry conforms to its security thresholds, the caching CMM returns it to the SDK. Otherwise, it tells the cache to evict the entry and proceeds as though there was no match.

   2. If the cache cannot find a valid match, the caching CMM asks its underlying CMM to generate a new data key.

      The CMM gets master keys (or objects that represent master keys) from its master key provider and it uses them to generate a new data key. This might involve a call to a service, such as AWS Key

Management Service. The CMM returns the plaintext and encrypted copies of the data key to the caching CMM.

The caching CMM saves the new data key in the cache.

4. The caching CMM returns plaintext and encrypted copies of the data key to the AWS Encryption SDK.

5. The AWS Encryption SDK uses the data key to encrypt the data and it returns an encrypted message to the user.

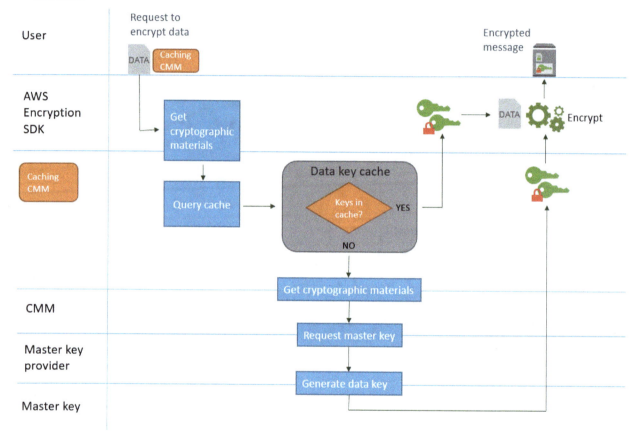

Creating a Cryptographic Materials Cache

The AWS Encryption SDK defines the requirements for a cryptographic materials cache used in data key caching. It also provides *LocalCryptoMaterialsCache*, a configurable, in-memory, least recently used (LRU) cache, and a null cryptographic materials cache for testing.

LocalCryptoMaterialsCache includes logic for basic cache management, including adding, evicting, and matching cached entries, and maintaining the cache. You don't need to write any custom cache management logic. You can use LocalCryptoMaterialsCache as is, customize it, or substitute any compatible cache.

When you create a LocalCryptoMaterialsCache, you set its *capacity*, that is, the maximum number of entries that the cache can hold. This setting helps you to design an efficient cache with limited data key reuse.

The AWS Encryption SDK also provides a *null cryptographic materials cache* (NullCryptoMaterialsCache). The NullCryptoMaterialsCache returns a miss for all get operations and does not respond to put operations. You can use the NullCryptoMaterialsCache in testing or to temporarily disable caching in an application that includes caching code.

In the AWS Encryption SDK, each cryptographic materials cache is associated with a caching cryptographic materials manager (caching CMM). The caching CMM gets data keys from the cache, puts data keys in the cache, and enforces security thresholds that you set. When you create a caching CMM, you specify the cache that it uses and the underlying CMM or master key provider that generates the data keys that it caches.

Creating a Caching Cryptographic Materials Manager

To enable data key caching, you create a cache and a *caching cryptographic materials manager* (caching CMM). Then, in your requests to encrypt or decrypt data, you specify a caching CMM, instead of a standard cryptographic materials manager (CMM) or master key provider .

There are two types of CMMs. Both get data keys (and related cryptographic material), but in different ways, as follows:

- A CMM is associated with a master key provider. When the SDK asks the CMM for data keys (get encryption materials), the CMM gets master keys (or objects that represent master keys) from its master key provider. Then, it uses the master keys to generate, encrypt, or decrypt the data keys.

- A caching CMM is associated with one cache, such as a LocalCryptoMaterialsCache, and a CMM or master key provider. (If you specify a master key provider, the SDK creates a default CMM for the master key provider.) When the SDK asks the caching CMM for data keys, the caching CMM tries to get them from the cache. If it cannot find a valid, matching data key, the caching CMM asks its underlying CMM for the data keys. Then, it caches those data keys before returning them to the caller.

The caching CMM also enforces security thresholds that you set for each cache entry. Because the security thresholds are set in and enforced by the caching CMM, you can use any compatible cache, even if the cache is not designed for sensitive material.

For details about creating and managing CMMs and caching CMMs in your application, see the SDK for your programming language.

What Is in a Data Key Cache Entry?

Data key caching stores data keys and related cryptographic materials in a cache. Each entry includes the elements listed below. You might find this information useful when you're deciding whether to use the data key caching feature, and when you're setting security thresholds on a caching cryptographic materials manager (caching CMM).

Cached Entries for Encryption Requests
The entries that are added to a data key cache as a result of a encryption operation include the following elements:

- Plaintext data key
- Encrypted data keys (one or more)
- Encryption context
- Message signing key (if one is used)
- Algorithm suite
- Metadata, including usage counters for enforcing security thresholds

Cached Entries for Decryption Requests
The entries that are added to a data key cache as a result of a decryption operation include the following elements:

- Plaintext data key
- Signature verification key (if one is used)
- Metadata, including usage counters for enforcing security thresholds

Encryption Context: How to Select Cache Entries

You can specify an encryption context in any request to encrypt data. However, the encryption context plays a special role in data key caching. It lets you create subgroups of data keys in your cache, even when the data keys originate from the same caching CMM.

An encryption context is a set of key-value pairs that contain arbitrary nonsecret data. During encryption, the encryption context is cryptographically bound to the encrypted data so that the same encryption context is required to decrypt the data. In the AWS Encryption SDK, the encryption context is stored in the encrypted message along with the encrypted data and data keys.

When you use a data key cache, you can also use the encryption context to select particular cached data keys for your encryption operations. The encryption context is saved in the cache entry with the data key (it's part of the cache entry ID). Cached data keys are reused only when their encryption contexts match. If you want to reuse certain data keys for an encryption request, specify the same encryption context. If you want to avoid those data keys, specify a different encryption context.

The encryption context is always optional, but recommended. If you don't specify an encryption context in your request, an empty encryption context is included in the cache entry identifier and matched to each request.

Data Key Caching Example

This example uses data key caching with a LocalCryptoMaterialsCache to speed up an application in which data generated by multiple devices is encrypted and stored in different regions.

In this scenario, multiple data producers generate data, encrypt it, and write to a Kinesis stream in each region. AWS Lambda functions (consumers) decrypt the streams and write plaintext data to a DynamoDB table in the region. Data producers and consumers use the AWS Encryption SDK and a KMS master key provider. To reduce calls to KMS, each producer and consumer has their own LocalCryptoMaterialsCache.

You can find the source code for these examples in Java and Python. The sample also includes a AWS CloudFormation template that defines the resources for the samples.

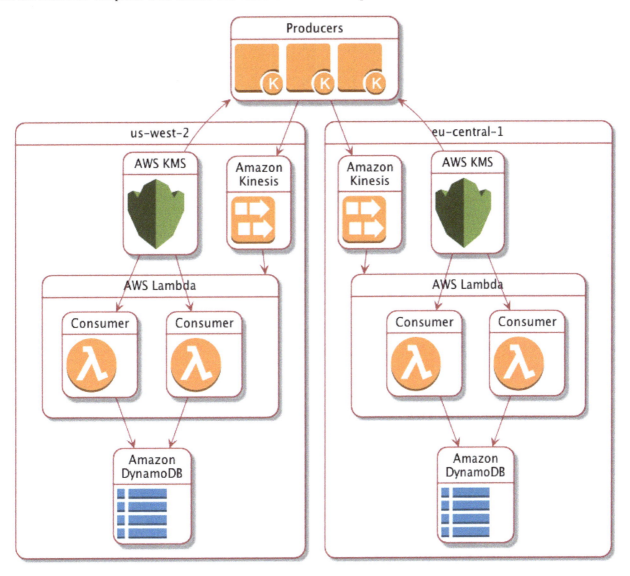

LocalCryptoMaterialsCache Results

The following table shows that LocalCryptoMaterialsCache reduces the total calls to KMS (per second per region) in this example to 1% of its original value.

Producer requests

[See the AWS documentation website for more details]

Consumer requests

[See the AWS documentation website for more details]

Data Key Caching Example in Java

This code sample creates a basic implementation of data key caching with a LocalCryptoMaterialsCache in Java. For details about the Java implementation of the AWS Encryption SDK, see AWS Encryption SDK for Java.

The code creates two instances of a LocalCryptoMaterialsCache; one for data producers that are encrypting data and another for data consumers (Lambda functions) that are decrypting data. For implementation details, see the Javadoc for the AWS Encryption SDK.

Producer

The producer gets a map, converts it to JSON, uses the AWS Encryption SDK to encrypt it, and pushes the ciphertext record to a Kinesis stream in each region.

The code defines a caching cryptographic materials manager (caching CMM) and associates it with a LocalCryptoMaterialsCache and an underlying KMS master key provider. The caching CMM caches the data keys (and related cryptographic materials) from the master key provider. It also interacts with the cache on behalf of the SDK and enforces security thresholds that you set.

Because the call to the `encryptData` method specifies a caching CMM, instead of a regular cryptographic materials manager (CMM) or master key provider, the method will use data key caching.

```
1  /*
2   * Copyright 2017 Amazon.com, Inc. or its affiliates. All Rights Reserved.
3   *
4   * Licensed under the Apache License, Version 2.0 (the "License"). You may not use this file
         except
5   * in compliance with the License. A copy of the License is located at
6   *
7   * http://aws.amazon.com/apache2.0
8   *
9   * or in the "license" file accompanying this file. This file is distributed on an "AS IS" BASIS
       ,
10  * WITHOUT WARRANTIES OR CONDITIONS OF ANY KIND, either express or implied. See the License for
         the
11  * specific language governing permissions and limitations under the License.
12  */
13 package com.amazonaws.crypto.examples.kinesisdatakeycaching;
14
15 import java.nio.ByteBuffer;
16 import java.util.ArrayList;
17 import java.util.HashMap;
18 import java.util.List;
19 import java.util.Map;
20 import java.util.UUID;
21 import java.util.concurrent.TimeUnit;
22
23 import com.amazonaws.ClientConfiguration;
24 import com.amazonaws.auth.DefaultAWSCredentialsProviderChain;
25 import com.amazonaws.encryptionsdk.AwsCrypto;
26 import com.amazonaws.encryptionsdk.CryptoResult;
27 import com.amazonaws.encryptionsdk.MasterKeyProvider;
28 import com.amazonaws.encryptionsdk.caching.CachingCryptoMaterialsManager;
29 import com.amazonaws.encryptionsdk.caching.LocalCryptoMaterialsCache;
30 import com.amazonaws.encryptionsdk.kms.KmsMasterKey;
```

```java
31 import com.amazonaws.encryptionsdk.kms.KmsMasterKeyProvider;
32 import com.amazonaws.encryptionsdk.multi.MultipleProviderFactory;
33 import com.amazonaws.regions.Region;
34 import com.amazonaws.services.kinesis.AmazonKinesis;
35 import com.amazonaws.services.kinesis.AmazonKinesisClientBuilder;
36 import com.amazonaws.util.json.Jackson;
37
38 /**
39  * Pushes data to Kinesis Streams in multiple regions.
40  */
41 public class MultiRegionRecordPusher {
42     private static long MAX_ENTRY_AGE_MILLISECONDS = 300000;
43     private static long MAX_ENTRY_USES = 100;
44     private static int MAX_CACHE_ENTRIES = 100;
45     private final String streamName_;
46     private ArrayList<AmazonKinesis> kinesisClients_;
47     private CachingCryptoMaterialsManager cachingMaterialsManager_;
48     private AwsCrypto crypto_;
49
50     /**
51      * Creates an instance of this object with Kinesis clients for all target regions
52      * and a cached key provider containing KMS master keys in all target regions.
53      */
54     public MultiRegionRecordPusher(final Region[] regions, final String kmsAliasName, final
             String streamName){
55         streamName_ = streamName;
56         crypto_ = new AwsCrypto();
57         kinesisClients_ = new ArrayList<AmazonKinesis>();
58
59         DefaultAWSCredentialsProviderChain credentialsProvider = new
                 DefaultAWSCredentialsProviderChain();
60         ClientConfiguration clientConfig = new ClientConfiguration();
61
62         // Build KmsMasterKey and AmazonKinesisClient objects for each target region
63         List<KmsMasterKey> masterKeys = new ArrayList<KmsMasterKey>();
64         for (Region region : regions) {
65             kinesisClients_.add(AmazonKinesisClientBuilder.standard()
66                     .withCredentials(credentialsProvider)
67                     .withRegion(region.getName())
68                     .build());
69
70             KmsMasterKey regionMasterKey = new KmsMasterKeyProvider(
71                 credentialsProvider,
72                 region,
73                 clientConfig,
74                 kmsAliasName
75             ).getMasterKey(kmsAliasName);
76
77             masterKeys.add(regionMasterKey);
78         }
79
80         // Collect KmsMasterKey objects into single provider and add cache
81         MasterKeyProvider<?> masterKeyProvider = MultipleProviderFactory.buildMultiProvider(
82                 KmsMasterKey.class,
```

```
83            masterKeys
84        );
85
86        cachingMaterialsManager_ = CachingCryptoMaterialsManager.newBuilder()
87            .withMasterKeyProvider(masterKeyProvider)
88            .withCache(new LocalCryptoMaterialsCache(MAX_CACHE_ENTRIES))
89            .withMaxAge(MAX_ENTRY_AGE_MILLISECONDS, TimeUnit.MILLISECONDS)
90            .withMessageUseLimit(MAX_ENTRY_USES)
91            .build();
92    }
93
94    /**
95     * JSON serializes and encrypts the received record data and pushes it to all target streams
         .
96     */
97    public void putRecord(final Map<Object, Object> data){
98        String partitionKey = UUID.randomUUID().toString();
99        Map<String, String> encryptionContext = new HashMap<String, String>();
100       encryptionContext.put("stream", streamName_);
101
102       // JSON serialize data
103       String jsonData = Jackson.toJsonString(data);
104
105       // Encrypt data
106       CryptoResult<byte[], ?> result = crypto_.encryptData(
107           cachingMaterialsManager_,
108           jsonData.getBytes(),
109           encryptionContext
110       );
111       byte[] encryptedData = result.getResult();
112
113       // Put records to Kinesis stream in all regions
114       for (AmazonKinesis regionalKinesisClient : kinesisClients_) {
115           regionalKinesisClient.putRecord(
116               streamName_,
117               ByteBuffer.wrap(encryptedData),
118               partitionKey
119           );
120       }
121   }
122 }
```

Consumer

The data consumer is an AWS Lambda function that is triggered by Kinesis events. It decrypts and deserializes each record, and writes the plaintext record to a DynamoDB table in the same region.

Like the producer code, the consumer code enables data key caching by using a caching cryptographic materials manager (caching CMM) in calls to the decryptData method.

```
1 /*
2  * Copyright 2017 Amazon.com, Inc. or its affiliates. All Rights Reserved.
3  *
4  * Licensed under the Apache License, Version 2.0 (the "License"). You may not use this file
     except
```

```
 5   * in compliance with the License. A copy of the License is located at
 6   *
 7   * http://aws.amazon.com/apache2.0
 8   *
 9   * or in the "license" file accompanying this file. This file is distributed on an "AS IS" BASIS
     ,
10   * WITHOUT WARRANTIES OR CONDITIONS OF ANY KIND, either express or implied. See the License for
     the
11   * specific language governing permissions and limitations under the License.
12   */
13  package com.amazonaws.crypto.examples.kinesisdatakeycaching;
14
15  import java.io.UnsupportedEncodingException;
16  import java.nio.ByteBuffer;
17  import java.util.concurrent.TimeUnit;
18
19  import com.amazonaws.encryptionsdk.AwsCrypto;
20  import com.amazonaws.encryptionsdk.CryptoResult;
21  import com.amazonaws.encryptionsdk.caching.CachingCryptoMaterialsManager;
22  import com.amazonaws.encryptionsdk.caching.LocalCryptoMaterialsCache;
23  import com.amazonaws.encryptionsdk.kms.KmsMasterKey;
24  import com.amazonaws.encryptionsdk.kms.KmsMasterKeyProvider;
25  import com.amazonaws.services.dynamodbv2.AmazonDynamoDBClientBuilder;
26  import com.amazonaws.services.dynamodbv2.document.DynamoDB;
27  import com.amazonaws.services.dynamodbv2.document.Item;
28  import com.amazonaws.services.dynamodbv2.document.Table;
29  import com.amazonaws.services.lambda.runtime.Context;
30  import com.amazonaws.services.lambda.runtime.events.KinesisEvent;
31  import com.amazonaws.services.lambda.runtime.events.KinesisEvent.KinesisEventRecord;
32  import com.amazonaws.util.BinaryUtils;
33
34  /**
35   * Decrypts all incoming Kinesis records and writes records to DynamoDB.
36   */
37  public class LambdaDecryptAndWrite {
38      private static final long MAX_ENTRY_AGE_MILLISECONDS = 600000;
39      private static final int MAX_CACHE_ENTRIES = 100;
40      private CachingCryptoMaterialsManager cachingMaterialsManager_;
41      private AwsCrypto crypto_;
42      private Table table_;
43
44      /**
45       * Because the cache is used only for decryption, the code doesn't set
46       * the max bytes or max message security thresholds that are are enforced
47       * only on on data keys used for encryption.
48       */
49      public LambdaDecryptAndWrite() {
50          String cmkArn = System.getenv("CMK_ARN");
51          cachingMaterialsManager_ = CachingCryptoMaterialsManager.newBuilder()
52              .withMasterKeyProvider(new KmsMasterKeyProvider(cmkArn))
53              .withCache(new LocalCryptoMaterialsCache(MAX_CACHE_ENTRIES))
54              .withMaxAge(MAX_ENTRY_AGE_MILLISECONDS, TimeUnit.MILLISECONDS)
55              .build();
56
```

```java
57      crypto_ = new AwsCrypto();
58      String tableName = System.getenv("TABLE_NAME");
59      DynamoDB dynamodb = new DynamoDB(AmazonDynamoDBClientBuilder.defaultClient());
60      table_ = dynamodb.getTable(tableName);
61  }
62
63  /**
64   *
65   * @param event
66   * @param context
67   */
68  public void handleRequest(KinesisEvent event, Context context) throws
        UnsupportedEncodingException{
69      for (KinesisEventRecord record : event.getRecords()) {
70          ByteBuffer ciphertextBuffer = record.getKinesis().getData();
71          byte[] ciphertext = BinaryUtils.copyAllBytesFrom(ciphertextBuffer);
72
73          // Decrypt and unpack record
74          CryptoResult<byte[], ?> plaintextResult = crypto_.decryptData(
                cachingMaterialsManager_, ciphertext);
75
76          // Verify the encryption context value
77          String streamArn = record.getEventSourceARN();
78          String streamName = streamArn.substring(streamArn.indexOf("/") + 1);
79          if (!streamName.equals(plaintextResult.getEncryptionContext().get("stream"))) {
80              throw new IllegalStateException("Wrong Encryption Context!");
81          }
82
83          // Write record to DynamoDB
84          String jsonItem = new String(plaintextResult.getResult(), "UTF-8");
85          System.out.println(jsonItem);
86          table_.putItem(Item.fromJSON(jsonItem));
87      }
88  }
89 }
```

Data Key Caching Example in Python

This code sample creates a basic implementation of data key caching with a LocalCryptoMaterialsCache in Python. For details about the Python implementation of the AWS Encryption SDK, see AWS Encryption SDK for Python.

The code creates two instances of a LocalCryptoMaterialsCache; one for data producers that are encrypting data and another for data consumers (Lambda functions) that are decrypting data. For implementation details, see the Python documentation for the AWS Encryption SDK.

Producer

The producer gets a map, converts it to JSON, uses the AWS Encryption SDK to encrypt it, and pushes the ciphertext record to an Kinesis stream in each region.

The code defines a caching cryptographic materials manager (caching CMM) and associates it with a LocalCryptoMaterialsCache and an underlying KMS master key provider. The caching CMM caches the data keys (and related cryptographic materials) from the master key provider. It also interacts with the cache on behalf of the SDK and enforces security thresholds that you set.

Because the call to the `encrypt` method specifies a caching CMM, instead of a regular cryptographic materials manager (CMM) or master key provider, the method will use data key caching.

```python
1  """
2  Copyright 2017 Amazon.com, Inc. or its affiliates. All Rights Reserved.
3
4  Licensed under the Apache License, Version 2.0 (the "License"). You may not use this file except
5  in compliance with the License. A copy of the License is located at
6
7  https://aws.amazon.com/apache-2-0/
8
9  or in the "license" file accompanying this file. This file is distributed on an "AS IS" BASIS,
10 WITHOUT WARRANTIES OR CONDITIONS OF ANY KIND, either express or implied. See the License for the
11 specific language governing permissions and limitations under the License.
12 """
13 import json
14 import uuid
15
16 from aws_encryption_sdk import encrypt, KMSMasterKeyProvider, CachingCryptoMaterialsManager,
       LocalCryptoMaterialsCache
17 from aws_encryption_sdk.key_providers.kms import KMSMasterKey
18 import boto3
19
20
21 class MultiRegionRecordPusher(object):
22     """Pushes data to Kinesis Streams in multiple regions."""
23     CACHE_CAPACITY = 100
24     MAX_ENTRY_AGE_SECONDS = 300.0
25     MAX_ENTRY_MESSAGES_ENCRYPTED = 100
26
27     def __init__(self, regions, kms_alias_name, stream_name):
28         self._kinesis_clients = []
29         self._stream_name = stream_name
30
31         # Set up KMSMasterKeyProvider with cache
```

```
32          _key_provider = KMSMasterKeyProvider()
33
34          # Add MasterKey and Kinesis client for each region
35          for region in regions:
36              self._kinesis_clients.append(boto3.client('kinesis', region_name=region))
37              regional_master_key = KMSMasterKey(
38                  client=boto3.client('kms', region_name=region),
39                  key_id=kms_alias_name
40              )
41              _key_provider.add_master_key_provider(regional_master_key)
42
43          cache = LocalCryptoMaterialsCache(capacity=self.CACHE_CAPACITY)
44          self._materials_manager = CachingCryptoMaterialsManager(
45              master_key_provider=_key_provider,
46              cache=cache,
47              max_age=self.MAX_ENTRY_AGE_SECONDS,
48              max_messages_encrypted=self.MAX_ENTRY_MESSAGES_ENCRYPTED
49          )
50
51      def put_record(self, record_data):
52          """JSON serializes and encrypts the received record data and pushes it to all target
                streams.
53
54          :param dict record_data: Data to write to stream
55          """
56          # Kinesis partition key to randomize write load across stream shards
57          partition_key = uuid.uuid4().hex
58
59          encryption_context = {'stream': self._stream_name}
60
61          # JSON serialize data
62          json_data = json.dumps(record_data)
63
64          # Encrypt data
65          encrypted_data, _header = encrypt(
66              source=json_data,
67              materials_manager=self._materials_manager,
68              encryption_context=encryption_context
69          )
70
71          # Put records to Kinesis stream in all regions
72          for client in self._kinesis_clients:
73              client.put_record(
74                  StreamName=self._stream_name,
75                  Data=encrypted_data,
76                  PartitionKey=partition_key
77              )
```

Consumer

The data consumer is an AWS Lambda function that is triggered by Kinesis events. It decrypts and deserializes each record, and writes the plaintext record to a DynamoDB table in the same region.

Like the producer code, the consumer code enables data key caching by using a caching cryptographic materials manager (caching CMM) in calls to the decrypt method.

```python
"""
Copyright 2017 Amazon.com, Inc. or its affiliates. All Rights Reserved.

Licensed under the Apache License, Version 2.0 (the "License"). You may not use this file except
in compliance with the License. A copy of the License is located at

https://aws.amazon.com/apache-2-0/

or in the "license" file accompanying this file. This file is distributed on an "AS IS" BASIS,
WITHOUT WARRANTIES OR CONDITIONS OF ANY KIND, either express or implied. See the License for the
specific language governing permissions and limitations under the License.
"""
import base64
import json
import logging
import os

from aws_encryption_sdk import decrypt, KMSMasterKeyProvider, CachingCryptoMaterialsManager,
    LocalCryptoMaterialsCache
import boto3

_LOGGER = logging.getLogger(__name__)
_is_setup = False
CACHE_CAPACITY = 100
MAX_ENTRY_AGE_SECONDS = 600.0

def setup():
    """Sets up clients that should persist across Lambda invocations."""
    global materials_manager
    key_provider = KMSMasterKeyProvider()
    cache = LocalCryptoMaterialsCache(capacity=CACHE_CAPACITY)

    #  Because the cache is used only for decryption, the code doesn't set
    #   the max bytes or max message security thresholds that are are enforced
    #   only on on data keys used for encryption.
    materials_manager = CachingCryptoMaterialsManager(
        master_key_provider=key_provider,
        cache=cache,
        max_age=MAX_ENTRY_AGE_SECONDS
    )
    global table
    table_name = os.environ.get('TABLE_NAME')
    table = boto3.resource('dynamodb').Table(table_name)
    global _is_setup
    _is_setup = True


def lambda_handler(event, context):
    """Decrypts all incoming Kinesis records and writes records to DynamoDB."""
    _LOGGER.debug('New event:')
    _LOGGER.debug(event)
    if not _is_setup:
        setup()
```

```
53    with table.batch_writer() as batch:
54        for record in event.get('Records', []):
55            # Record data base64-encoded by Kinesis
56            ciphertext = base64.b64decode(record['kinesis']['data'])
57
58            # Decrypt and unpack record
59            plaintext, header = decrypt(
60                source=ciphertext,
61                materials_manager=materials_manager
62            )
63            item = json.loads(plaintext)
64
65            # Verify the encryption context value
66            stream_name = record['eventSourceARN'].split('/', 1)[1]
67            if stream_name != header.encryption_context['stream']:
68                raise ValueError('Wrong Encryption Context!')
69
70            # Write record to DynamoDB
71            batch.put_item(Item=item)
```

LocalCryptoMaterialsCache Example AWS CloudFormation Template

This AWS CloudFormation template sets up all the necessary AWS resources to replicate this example.

```
1  Parameters:
2      SourceCodeBucket:
3          Type: String
4          Description: S3 bucket containing Lambda source code zip files
5      PythonLambdaS3Key:
6          Type: String
7          Description: S3 key containing Python Lambda source code zip file
8      PythonLambdaObjectVersionId:
9          Type: String
10         Description: S3 version id for S3 key containing Python Lambda source code zip file
11     JavaLambdaS3Key:
12         Type: String
13         Description: S3 key containing Python Lambda source code zip file
14     JavaLambdaObjectVersionId:
15         Type: String
16         Description: S3 version id for S3 key containing Python Lambda source code zip file
17     KeyAliasSuffix:
18         Type: String
19         Description: 'Suffix to use for KMS CMK Alias (ie: alias/<KeyAliasSuffix>)'
20     StreamName:
21         Type: String
22         Description: Name to use for Kinesis Stream
23 Resources:
24     InputStream:
25         Type: AWS::Kinesis::Stream
26         Properties:
27             Name: !Ref StreamName
28             ShardCount: 2
29     PythonLambdaOutputTable:
30         Type: AWS::DynamoDB::Table
31         Properties:
32             AttributeDefinitions:
33                 -
34                     AttributeName: id
35                     AttributeType: S
36             KeySchema:
37                 -
38                     AttributeName: id
39                     KeyType: HASH
40             ProvisionedThroughput:
41                 ReadCapacityUnits: 1
42                 WriteCapacityUnits: 1
43     PythonLambdaRole:
44         Type: AWS::IAM::Role
45         Properties:
46             AssumeRolePolicyDocument:
47                 Version: 2012-10-17
48                 Statement:
49                     -
```

```yaml
50                        Effect: Allow
51                        Principal:
52                            Service: lambda.amazonaws.com
53                        Action: sts:AssumeRole
54                ManagedPolicyArns:
55                    - arn:aws:iam::aws:policy/service-role/AWSLambdaBasicExecutionRole
56                Policies:
57                    -
58                        PolicyName: PythonLambdaAccess
59                        PolicyDocument:
60                            Version: 2012-10-17
61                            Statement:
62                                -
63                                    Effect: Allow
64                                    Action:
65                                        - dynamodb:DescribeTable
66                                        - dynamodb:BatchWriteItem
67                                    Resource: !Sub arn:aws:dynamodb:${AWS::Region}:${AWS::AccountId
                                        }:table/${PythonLambdaOutputTable}
68                                -
69                                    Effect: Allow
70                                    Action:
71                                        - dynamodb:PutItem
72                                    Resource: !Sub arn:aws:dynamodb:${AWS::Region}:${AWS::AccountId
                                        }:table/${PythonLambdaOutputTable}*
73                                -
74                                    Effect: Allow
75                                    Action:
76                                        - kinesis:GetRecords
77                                        - kinesis:GetShardIterator
78                                        - kinesis:DescribeStream
79                                        - kinesis:ListStreams
80                                    Resource: !Sub arn:aws:kinesis:${AWS::Region}:${AWS::AccountId}:
                                        stream/${InputStream}
81    PythonLambdaFunction:
82        Type: AWS::Lambda::Function
83        Properties:
84            Description: Python consumer
85            Runtime: python2.7
86            MemorySize: 512
87            Timeout: 90
88            Role: !GetAtt PythonLambdaRole.Arn
89            Handler: aws_crypto_examples.kinesis_datakey_caching.consumer.lambda_handler
90            Code:
91                S3Bucket: !Ref SourceCodeBucket
92                S3Key: !Ref PythonLambdaS3Key
93                S3ObjectVersion: !Ref PythonLambdaObjectVersionId
94            Environment:
95                Variables:
96                    TABLE_NAME: !Ref PythonLambdaOutputTable
97    PythonLambdaSourceMapping:
98        Type: AWS::Lambda::EventSourceMapping
99        Properties:
100            BatchSize: 1
```

```yaml
101             Enabled: true
102             EventSourceArn: !Sub arn:aws:kinesis:${AWS::Region}:${AWS::AccountId}:stream/${
                    InputStream}
103             FunctionName: !Ref PythonLambdaFunction
104             StartingPosition: TRIM_HORIZON
105       JavaLambdaOutputTable:
106         Type: AWS::DynamoDB::Table
107         Properties:
108           AttributeDefinitions:
109             -
110                 AttributeName: id
111                 AttributeType: S
112           KeySchema:
113             -
114                 AttributeName: id
115                 KeyType: HASH
116           ProvisionedThroughput:
117             ReadCapacityUnits: 1
118             WriteCapacityUnits: 1
119       JavaLambdaRole:
120         Type: AWS::IAM::Role
121         Properties:
122           AssumeRolePolicyDocument:
123             Version: 2012-10-17
124             Statement:
125               -
126                   Effect: Allow
127                   Principal:
128                     Service: lambda.amazonaws.com
129                   Action: sts:AssumeRole
130           ManagedPolicyArns:
131             - arn:aws:iam::aws:policy/service-role/AWSLambdaBasicExecutionRole
132           Policies:
133             -
134                 PolicyName: JavaLambdaAccess
135                 PolicyDocument:
136                   Version: 2012-10-17
137                   Statement:
138                     -
139                         Effect: Allow
140                         Action:
141                           - dynamodb:DescribeTable
142                           - dynamodb:BatchWriteItem
143                         Resource: !Sub arn:aws:dynamodb:${AWS::Region}:${AWS::AccountId
                              }:table/${JavaLambdaOutputTable}
144                     -
145                         Effect: Allow
146                         Action:
147                           - dynamodb:PutItem
148                         Resource: !Sub arn:aws:dynamodb:${AWS::Region}:${AWS::AccountId
                              }:table/${JavaLambdaOutputTable}*
149                     -
150                         Effect: Allow
151                         Action:
```

```yaml
152                                    - kinesis:GetRecords
153                                    - kinesis:GetShardIterator
154                                    - kinesis:DescribeStream
155                                    - kinesis:ListStreams
156                             Resource: !Sub arn:aws:kinesis:${AWS::Region}:${AWS::AccountId}:
                                    stream/${InputStream}
157      JavaLambdaFunction:
158          Type: AWS::Lambda::Function
159          Properties:
160              Description: Java consumer
161              Runtime: java8
162              MemorySize: 512
163              Timeout: 90
164              Role: !GetAtt JavaLambdaRole.Arn
165              Handler: com.amazonaws.crypto.examples.kinesisdatakeycaching.LambdaDecryptAndWrite::
                    handleRequest
166              Code:
167                  S3Bucket: !Ref SourceCodeBucket
168                  S3Key: !Ref JavaLambdaS3Key
169                  S3ObjectVersion: !Ref JavaLambdaObjectVersionId
170              Environment:
171                  Variables:
172                      TABLE_NAME: !Ref JavaLambdaOutputTable
173                      CMK_ARN: !GetAtt RegionKinesisCMK.Arn
174      JavaLambdaSourceMapping:
175          Type: AWS::Lambda::EventSourceMapping
176          Properties:
177              BatchSize: 1
178              Enabled: true
179              EventSourceArn: !Sub arn:aws:kinesis:${AWS::Region}:${AWS::AccountId}:stream/${
                    InputStream}
180              FunctionName: !Ref JavaLambdaFunction
181              StartingPosition: TRIM_HORIZON
182      RegionKinesisCMK:
183          Type: AWS::KMS::Key
184          Properties:
185              Description: Used to encrypt data passing through Kinesis Stream in this region
186              Enabled: true
187              KeyPolicy:
188                  Version: 2012-10-17
189                  Statement:
190                      -
191                          Effect: Allow
192                          Principal:
193                              AWS: !Sub arn:aws:iam::${AWS::AccountId}:root
194                          Action:
195                              # Data plane actions
196                              - kms:Encrypt
197                              - kms:GenerateDataKey
198                              # Control plane actions
199                              - kms:CreateAlias
200                              - kms:DeleteAlias
201                              - kms:DescribeKey
202                              - kms:DisableKey
```

```
203                              - kms:EnableKey
204                              - kms:PutKeyPolicy
205                              - kms:ScheduleKeyDeletion
206                              - kms:UpdateAlias
207                              - kms:UpdateKeyDescription
208                    Resource: '*'
209                 -
210                    Effect: Allow
211                    Principal:
212                      AWS:
213                        - !GetAtt PythonLambdaRole.Arn
214                        - !GetAtt JavaLambdaRole.Arn
215                    Action: kms:Decrypt
216                    Resource: '*'
217    RegionKinesisCMKAlias:
218       Type: AWS::KMS::Alias
219       Properties:
220         AliasName: !Sub alias/${KeyAliasSuffix}
221         TargetKeyId: !Ref RegionKinesisCMK
```

Frequently Asked Questions

- How is the AWS Encryption SDK different from the AWS SDKs?
- How is the AWS Encryption SDK different from the Amazon S3 encryption client?
- Which cryptographic algorithms are supported by the AWS Encryption SDK, and which one is the default?
- How is the initialization vector (IV) generated and where is it stored?
- How is each data key generated, encrypted, and decrypted?
- How do I keep track of the data keys that were used to encrypt my data?
- How does the AWS Encryption SDK store encrypted data keys with their encrypted data?
- How much overhead does the AWS Encryption SDK's message format add to my encrypted data?
- Can I use my own master key provider?
- Can I encrypt data under more than one master key?
- Which data types can I encrypt with the AWS Encryption SDK?
- How does the AWS Encryption SDK encrypt and decrypt input/output (I/O) streams?

How is the AWS Encryption SDK different from the AWS SDKs? The AWS SDKs provide libraries for interacting with Amazon Web Services (AWS). They integrate with AWS Key Management Service (AWS KMS) to generate, encrypt, and decrypt data keys. However, in most cases you can't use them to directly encrypt or decrypt raw data.

The AWS Encryption SDK provides an encryption library that optionally integrates with AWS KMS as a master key provider. The AWS Encryption SDK builds on the AWS SDKs to do the following things:

- Generate, encrypt, and decrypt data keys
- Use those data keys to encrypt and decrypt your raw data
- Store the encrypted data keys with the corresponding encrypted data in a single object You can also use the AWS Encryption SDK with no AWS integration by defining a custom master key provider.

How is the AWS Encryption SDK different from the Amazon S3 encryption client? The Amazon S3 encryption client in the AWS SDK for Java, AWS SDK for Ruby, and AWS SDK for .NET provides encryption and decryption for data that you store in Amazon Simple Storage Service (Amazon S3). These clients are tightly coupled to Amazon S3 and are intended for use only with data stored there.

The AWS Encryption SDK provides encryption and decryption for data that you can store anywhere. The AWS Encryption SDK and the Amazon S3 encryption client are not compatible because they produce ciphertexts with different data formats.

Which cryptographic algorithms are supported by the AWS Encryption SDK, and which one is the default? The AWS Encryption SDK uses the Advanced Encryption Standard (AES) algorithm in Galois/Counter Mode (GCM), known as AES-GCM. The SDK supports 256-bit, 192-bit, and 128-bit encryption keys. In all cases, the length of the initialization vector (IV) is 12 bytes; the length of the authentication tag is 16 bytes. By default, the SDK uses the data key as an input to the HMAC-based extract-and-expand key derivation function (HKDF) to derive the AES-GCM encryption key, and also adds an Elliptic Curve Digital Signature Algorithm (ECDSA) signature.

For information about choosing which algorithm to use, see Supported Algorithm Suites.

For implementation details about the supported algorithms, see Algorithms Reference.

How is the initialization vector (IV) generated and where is it stored? In previous releases, the AWS Encryption SDK randomly generated a unique IV value for each encryption operation. The SDK now uses a deterministic method to construct a different IV value for each frame so that every IV is unique within its message. The SDK stores the IV in the encrypted message that it returns. For more information, see AWS Encryption SDK Message Format Reference.

How is each data key generated, encrypted, and decrypted? The method depends on the master key provider and the implementation of its master keys. When AWS KMS is the master key provider, the SDK uses the AWS KMS GenerateDataKey API operation to generate each data key in both plaintext and encrypted forms. It uses the Decrypt operation to decrypt the data key. AWS KMS encrypts and decrypts the data key by using the customer master key (CMK) that you specified when configuring the master key provider.

How do I keep track of the data keys that were used to encrypt my data? The AWS Encryption SDK does this for you. When you encrypt data, the SDK encrypts the data key and stores the encrypted key along with the encrypted data in the encrypted message that it returns. When you decrypt data, the AWS Encryption SDK extracts the encrypted data key from the encrypted method, decrypts it, and then uses it to decrypt the data.

How does the AWS Encryption SDK store encrypted data keys with their encrypted data? The encryption operations in the AWS Encryption SDK return an encrypted message, a single data structure that contains the encrypted data and its encrypted data keys. The message format consists of at least two parts: a *header* and a *body*. In some cases, the message format consists of a third part known as a *footer*. The message header contains the encrypted data keys and information about how the message body is formed. The message body contains the encrypted data. The message footer contains a signature that authenticates the message header and message body. For more information, see AWS Encryption SDK Message Format Reference.

How much overhead does the AWS Encryption SDK's message format add to my encrypted data? The amount of overhead added by the AWS Encryption SDK depends on several factors, including the following:

- The size of the plaintext data
- Which of the supported algorithms is used
- Whether additional authenticated data (AAD) is provided, and the length of that AAD
- The number and type of master key providers
- The frame size (when framed data is used) When you use the AWS Encryption SDK with its default configuration, with one CMK in AWS KMS as the master key, with no AAD, and encrypt nonframed data, the overhead is approximately 600 bytes. In general, you can reasonably assume that the AWS Encryption SDK adds overhead of 1 KB or less, not including the provided AAD. For more information, see AWS Encryption SDK Message Format Reference.

Can I use my own master key provider? Yes. The implementation details vary depending on which of the supported programming languages you use. However, all supported languages allow you to define custom cryptographic materials managers (CMMs), master key providers, and master keys.

Can I encrypt data under more than one master key? Yes. You can encrypt the data key with additional master keys to add redundancy in case a master key is in a different region or is unavailable for decryption.

To encrypt data under multiple master keys, create a master key provider with multiple master keys. You can see examples of this pattern in the example code for Java and Python.

When you encrypt data by using a master key provider that returns multiple master keys, the AWS Encryption SDK encrypts the data that you pass to the encryption methods with a data key and encrypts that data key with the same master key. Then, it encrypts the data with the other master keys that the master key provider returned. The resulting message includes the encrypted data and one encrypted data key for each master key. The resulting message can be decrypted by using any one of the master keys used in the encryption operation.

Which data types can I encrypt with the AWS Encryption SDK? The AWS Encryption SDK can encrypt raw bytes (byte arrays), I/O streams (byte streams), and strings. We provide example code for each of the supported programming languages.

How does the AWS Encryption SDK encrypt and decrypt input/output (I/O) streams? The AWS Encryption SDK creates an encrypting or decrypting stream that wraps an underlying I/O stream. The encrypting or decrypting stream performs a cryptographic operation on a read or write call. For example, it can read plaintext data on the underlying stream and encrypt it before returning the result. Or it can read ciphertext from an underlying stream and decrypt it before returning the result. We provide example code for encrypting and decrypting streams for each of the supported programming languages.

AWS Encryption SDK Reference

The information on this page is a reference for building your own encryption library that is compatible with the AWS Encryption SDK. If you are not building your own compatible encryption library, you likely do not need this information. To use the AWS Encryption SDK in one of the supported programming languages, see Programming Languages.

The AWS Encryption SDK uses the supported algorithms to return a single data structure or *message* that contains encrypted data and the corresponding encrypted data keys. The following topics explain the algorithms and the data structure. Use this information to build libraries that can read and write ciphertexts that are compatible with this SDK.

Topics

- Message Format Reference
- Body AAD Reference
- Message Format Examples
- Algorithms Reference
- Initialization Vector Reference

AWS Encryption SDK Message Format Reference

> The information on this page is a reference for building your own encryption library that is compatible with the AWS Encryption SDK. If you are not building your own compatible encryption library, you likely do not need this information. To use the AWS Encryption SDK in one of the supported programming languages, see Programming Languages.

The encryption operations in the AWS Encryption SDK return a single data structure or *message* that contains the encrypted data (ciphertext) and all encrypted data keys. To understand this data structure, or to build libraries that read and write it, you need to understand the message format.

The message format consists of at least two parts: a *header* and a *body*. In some cases, the message format consists of a third part, a *footer*. The message format defines an ordered sequence of bytes in network byte order, also called big-endian format. The message format begins with the header, followed by the body, followed by the footer (when there is one).

Topics

- Header Structure
- Body Structure
- Footer Structure

Header Structure

The message header contains the encrypted data key and information about how the message body is formed. The following table describes the fields that form the header. The bytes are appended in the order shown.

Header Structure

Field	Length, in bytes
Version	1
Type	1
Algorithm ID	2
Message ID	16
AAD Length	2
AAD	Variable. Equal to the value specified in the previous 2 bytes (AAD Length).
Encrypted Data Key Count	2
Encrypted Data Key(s)	Variable. Determined by the number of encrypted data keys and the length of each.
Content Type	1
Reserved	4
IV Length	1
Frame Length	4
Header Authentication	Variable. Determined by the algorithm that generated the message.

Version The version of this message format. The current version is 1.0, encoded as the byte 01 in hexadecimal notation.

Type The type of this message format. The type indicates the kind of structure. The only supported type is described as *customer authenticated encrypted data*. Its type value is 128, encoded as byte 80 in hexadecimal notation.

Algorithm ID An identifier for the algorithm used. It is a 2-byte value interpreted as a 16-bit unsigned integer. For more information about the algorithms, see AWS Encryption SDK Algorithms Reference.

Message ID A randomly generated 128-bit value that identifies the message. The Message ID:

- Uniquely identifies the encrypted message.
- Weakly binds the message header to the message body.
- Provides a mechanism to securely reuse a data key with multiple encrypted messages.
- Protects against accidental reuse of a data key or the wearing out of keys in the AWS Encryption SDK.

AAD Length The length of the additional authenticated data (AAD). It is a 2-byte value interpreted as a 16-bit unsigned integer that specifies the number of bytes that contain the AAD.

AAD The additional authenticated data. The AAD is an encoding of the encryption context, an array of key-value pairs where each key and value is a string of UTF-8 encoded characters. The encryption context is converted to a sequence of bytes and used for the AAD value.

When the algorithms with signing are used, the encryption context must contain the key-value pair {'aws-crypto-public-key', Qtxt}. Qtxt represents the elliptic curve point Q compressed according to SEC 1 version 2.0 and then base64-encoded. The encryption context can contain additional values, but the maximum length of the constructed AAD is $2^{16} - 1$ bytes.

The following table describes the fields that form the AAD. Key-value pairs are sorted, by key, in ascending order according to UTF-8 character code. The bytes are appended in the order shown.

AAD Structure

[See the AWS documentation website for more details]

Key-Value Pair Count The number of key-value pairs in the AAD. It is a 2-byte value interpreted as a 16-bit unsigned integer that specifies the number of key-value pairs in the AAD. The maximum number of key-value pairs in the AAD is $2^{16} - 1$.

Key Length The length of the key for the key-value pair. It is a 2-byte value interpreted as a 16-bit unsigned integer that specifies the number of bytes that contain the key.

Key The key for the key-value pair. It is a sequence of UTF-8 encoded bytes.

Value Length The length of the value for the key-value pair. It is a 2-byte value interpreted as a 16-bit unsigned integer that specifies the number of bytes that contain the value.

Value The value for the key-value pair. It is a sequence of UTF-8 encoded bytes.

Encrypted Data Key Count The number of encrypted data keys. It is a 2-byte value interpreted as a 16-bit unsigned integer that specifies the number of encrypted data keys.

Encrypted Data Key(s) A sequence of encrypted data keys. The length of the sequence is determined by the number of encrypted data keys and the length of each. The sequence contains at least one encrypted data key. The following table describes the fields that form each encrypted data key. The bytes are appended in the order shown.

Encrypted Data Key Structure

[See the AWS documentation website for more details]

Key Provider ID Length The length of the key provider identifier. It is a 2-byte value interpreted as a 16-bit unsigned integer that specifies the number of bytes that contain the key provider ID.

Key Provider ID The key provider identifier. It is used to indicate the provider of the encrypted data key and intended to be extensible.

Key Provider Information Length The length of the key provider information. It is a 2-byte value interpreted as a 16-bit unsigned integer that specifies the number of bytes that contain the key provider information.

Key Provider Information The key provider information. It is determined by the key provider.

When AWS KMS is the key provider, the following are true:

- This value contains the Amazon Resource Name (ARN) of the AWS KMS customer master key (CMK).
- This value is always the full CMK ARN, regardless of which key identifier (key ID, alias, etc.) was specified when calling the master key provider.

Encrypted Data Key Length The length of the encrypted data key. It is a 2-byte value interpreted as a 16-bit unsigned integer that specifies the number of bytes that contain the encrypted data key.

Encrypted Data Key The encrypted data key. It is the data encryption key encrypted by the key provider.

Content Type The type of encrypted content, either non-framed or framed.

Non-framed content is not broken into parts; it is a single encrypted blob. Non-framed content is type 1, encoded as the byte 01 in hexadecimal notation.

Framed content is broken into equal-length parts; each part is encrypted separately. Framed content is type 2, encoded as the byte 02 in hexadecimal notation.

Reserved A reserved sequence of 4 bytes. This value must be 0. It is encoded as the bytes 00 00 00 00 in hexadecimal notation (that is, a 4-byte sequence of a 32-bit integer value equal to 0).

IV Length The length of the initialization vector (IV). It is a 1-byte value interpreted as an 8-bit unsigned integer that specifies the number of bytes that contain the IV. This value is determined by the IV bytes value of the algorithm that generated the message.

Frame Length The length of each frame of framed content. It is a 4-byte value interpreted as a 32-bit unsigned integer that specifies the number of bytes that form each frame. When the content is non-framed—that is, when the value of the content type field is 1—this value must be 0.

Header Authentication The header authentication is determined by the algorithm that generated the message. The header authentication is calculated over the entire header. It consists of an IV and an authentication tag. The bytes are appended in the order shown.

Header Authentication Structure

[See the AWS documentation website for more details]

IV The initialization vector (IV) used to calculate the header authentication tag.

Authentication Tag The authentication value for the header. It is used to authenticate the entire contents of the header.

Body Structure

The message body contains the encrypted data, called the *ciphertext*. The structure of the body depends on the content type (non-framed or framed). The following sections describe the format of the message body for each content type.

Topics

- Non-Framed Data
- Framed Data

Non-Framed Data

Non-framed data is encrypted in a single blob with a unique IV and body AAD. The following table describes the fields that form non-framed data. The bytes are appended in the order shown.

Non-Framed Body Structure

Field	Length, in bytes
IV	Variable. Equal to the value specified in the IV Length byte of the header.
Encrypted Content Length	8
Encrypted Content	Variable. Equal to the value specified in the previous 8 bytes (Encrypted Content Length).
Authentication Tag	Variable. Determined by the algorithm implementation used.

IV The initialization vector (IV) to use with the encryption algorithm.

Encrypted Content Length The length of the encrypted content, or *ciphertext*. It is an 8-byte value interpreted as a 64-bit unsigned integer that specifies the number of bytes that contain the encrypted content.
Technically, the maximum allowed value is $2^{63} - 1$, or 8 exbibytes (8 EiB). However, in practice the maximum value is $2^{36} - 32$, or 64 gibibytes (64 GiB), due to restrictions imposed by the implemented algorithms.
The Java implementation of this SDK further restricts this value to $2^{31} - 1$, or 2 gibibytes (2 GiB), due to restrictions in the language.

Encrypted Content The encrypted content (ciphertext) as returned by the encryption algorithm.

Authentication Tag The authentication value for the body. It is used to authenticate the message body.

Framed Data

Framed data is divided into equal-length parts, except for the last part. Each frame is encrypted separately with a unique IV and body AAD.

There are two kinds of frames: regular and final. A final frame is always used. When the length of the data is an exact multiple of the frame length, the final frame contains no data—that is, it has a content length of 0. When the length of the data is less than the frame length, only a final frame is written.

The following tables describe the fields that form the frames. The bytes are appended in the order shown.

Framed Body Structure, Regular Frame

Field	Length, in bytes
Sequence Number	4
IV	Variable. Equal to the value specified in the IV Length byte of the header.
Encrypted Content	Variable. Equal to the value specified in the Frame Length of the header.
Authentication Tag	Variable. Determined by the algorithm used, as specified in the Algorithm ID of the header.

Sequence Number The frame sequence number. It is an incremental counter number for the frame. It is a 4-byte value interpreted as a 32-bit unsigned integer.
Framed data must start at sequence number 1. Subsequent frames must be in order and must contain an increment of 1 of the previous frame. Otherwise, the decryption process stops and reports an error.

IV The initialization vector (IV) for the frame. The SDK uses a deterministic method to construct a different IV for each frame in the message. Its length is specified by the algorithm suite used.

Encrypted Content The encrypted content (ciphertext) for the frame, as returned by the encryption algorithm.

Authentication Tag The authentication value for the frame. It is used to authenticate the entire frame.

Framed Body Structure, Final Frame

Field	Length, in bytes
Sequence Number End	4
Sequence Number	4
IV	Variable. Equal to the value specified in the IV Length byte of the header.
Encrypted Content Length	4
Encrypted Content	Variable. Equal to the value specified in the previous 4 bytes (Encrypted Content Length).

Field	Length, in bytes
Authentication Tag	Variable. Determined by the algorithm used, as specified in the Algorithm ID of the header.

Sequence Number End An indicator for the final frame. The value is encoded as the 4 bytes `FF FF FF FF` in hexadecimal notation.

Sequence Number The frame sequence number. It is an incremental counter number for the frame. It is a 4-byte value interpreted as a 32-bit unsigned integer.
Framed data must start at sequence number 1. Subsequent frames must be in order and must contain an increment of 1 of the previous frame. Otherwise, the decryption process stops and reports an error.

IV The initialization vector (IV) for the frame. The SDK uses a deterministic method to construct a different IV for each frame in the message. The length of the IV length is specified by the algorithm suite.

Encrypted Content Length The length of the encrypted content. It is a 4-byte value interpreted as a 32-bit unsigned integer that specifies the number of bytes that contain the encrypted content for the frame.

Encrypted Content The encrypted content (ciphertext) for the frame, as returned by the encryption algorithm.

Authentication Tag The authentication value for the frame. It is used to authenticate the entire frame.

Footer Structure

When the algorithms with signing are used, the message format contains a footer. The message footer contains a signature calculated over the message header and body. The following table describes the fields that form the footer. The bytes are appended in the order shown.

Footer Structure

Field	Length, in bytes
Signature Length	2
Signature	Variable. Equal to the value specified in the previous 2 bytes (Signature Length).

Signature Length The length of the signature. It is a 2-byte value interpreted as a 16-bit unsigned integer that specifies the number of bytes that contain the signature.

Signature The signature. It is used to authenticate the header and body of the message.

Body Additional Authenticated Data (AAD) Reference for the AWS Encryption SDK

> The information on this page is a reference for building your own encryption library that is compatible with the AWS Encryption SDK. If you are not building your own compatible encryption library, you likely do not need this information. To use the AWS Encryption SDK in one of the supported programming languages, see Programming Languages.

Regardless of which type of body data is used to form the message body (non-framed or framed), you must provide additional authenticated data (AAD) to the AES-GCM algorithm for each cryptographic operation. For more information about AAD, see the definition section in the Galois/Counter Mode of Operation (GCM) specification.

The following table describes the fields that form the body AAD. The bytes are appended in the order shown.

Body AAD Structure

Field	Length, in bytes
Message ID	16
Body AAD Content	Variable. See Body AAD Content in the following list.
Sequence Number	4
Content Length	8

Message ID The same Message ID value set in the message header.

Body AAD Content A UTF-8 encoded value determined by the type of body data used.
For non-framed data, use the value `AWSKMSEncryptionClient Single Block`.
For regular frames in framed data, use the value `AWSKMSEncryptionClient Frame`.
For the final frame in framed data, use the value `AWSKMSEncryptionClient Final Frame`.

Sequence Number A 4-byte value interpreted as a 32-bit unsigned integer.
For framed data, this is the frame sequence number.
For non-framed data, use the value 1, encoded as the 4 bytes `00 00 00 01` in hexadecimal notation.

Content Length The length, in bytes, of the plaintext data provided to the algorithm for encryption. It is an 8-byte value interpreted as a 64-bit unsigned integer.

AWS Encryption SDK Message Format Examples

> The information on this page is a reference for building your own encryption library that is compatible with the AWS Encryption SDK. If you are not building your own compatible encryption library, you likely do not need this information. To use the AWS Encryption SDK in one of the supported programming languages, see Programming Languages.

The following topics show examples of the AWS Encryption SDK message format. Each example shows the raw bytes, in hexadecimal notation, followed by a description of what those bytes represent.

Topics

- Non-Framed Data
- Framed Data

Non-Framed Data

The following example shows the message format for non-framed data.

```
1  +--------+
2  | Header |
3  +--------+
4  01                                        Version (1.0)
5  80                                        Type (128, customer authenticated encrypted data)
6  0378                                      Algorithm ID (see [Algorithms Reference](algorithms-
       reference.md))
7  B8929B01 753D4A45 C0217F39 404F70FF       Message ID (random 128-bit value)
8  008E                                      AAD Length (142)
9  0004                                      AAD Key-Value Pair Count (4)
10 0005                                      AAD Key-Value Pair 1, Key Length (5)
11 30746869 73                               AAD Key-Value Pair 1, Key ("0This")
12 0002                                      AAD Key-Value Pair 1, Value Length (2)
13 6973                                      AAD Key-Value Pair 1, Value ("is")
14 0003                                      AAD Key-Value Pair 2, Key Length (3)
15 31616E                                    AAD Key-Value Pair 2, Key ("1an")
16 000A                                      AAD Key-Value Pair 2, Value Length (10)
17 656E6372 79774690 6F6E                    AAD Key-Value Pair 2, Value ("encryption")
18 0008                                      AAD Key-Value Pair 3, Key Length (8)
19 32636F6E 74657874                         AAD Key-Value Pair 3, Key ("2context")
20 0007                                      AAD Key-Value Pair 3, Value Length (7)
21 6578616D 706C65                           AAD Key-Value Pair 3, Value ("example")
22 0015                                      AAD Key-Value Pair 4, Key Length (21)
23 6177732D 63727970 746F2D70 75626C69       AAD Key-Value Pair 4, Key ("aws-crypto-public-key")
24 632D6B65 79
25 0044                                      AAD Key-Value Pair 4, Value Length (68)
26 41734738 67473949 6E4C5075 3136594B       AAD Key-Value Pair 4, Value ("AsG8gG9InLPu16YKlqXTOD+
       nykG8YqHAhqecj8aXfD2e5B4gtVE73dZkyClA+rAMOQ==")
27 6C715854 4F442B6E 796B4738 59714841
28 68716563 6A386158 66443265 35423467
29 74564537 33645A6B 79436C41 2B72414D
30 4F513D3D
31 0002                                      Encrypted Data Key Count (2)
32 0007                                      Encrypted Data Key 1, Key Provider ID Length (7)
```

```
33 6177732D 6B6D73          Encrypted Data Key 1, Key Provider ID ("aws-kms")
34 004B                      Encrypted Data Key 1, Key Provider Information Length
      (75)
35 61726E3A 6177733A 6B6D733A 75732D77   Encrypted Data Key 1, Key Provider Information ("arn:
      aws:kms:us-west-2:111122223333:key/715c0818-5825-4245-a755-138a6d9a11e6")
36 6573742D 323A3131 31313232 32323333
37 33333A6B 65792F37 31356330 3831382D
38 35383235 2D343234 352D6137 35352D31
39 33386136 64396131 316536
40 00A7                      Encrypted Data Key 1, Encrypted Data Key Length (167)
41 01010200 7857A1C1 F7370545 4ECA7C83   Encrypted Data Key 1, Encrypted Data Key
42 956C4702 23DCE8D7 16C59679 973E3CED
43 02A4EF29 7F000000 7E307C06 092A8648
44 86F70D01 0706A06F 306D0201 00306806
45 092A8648 86F70D01 0701301E 06096086
46 48016503 04012E30 11040C28 4116449A
47 0F2A0383 659EF802 0110803B B23A8133
48 3A33605C 48840656 C38BCB1F 9CCE7369
49 E9A33EBE 33F46461 0591FECA 947262F3
50 418E1151 21311A75 E575ECC5 61A286E0
51 3E2DEBD5 CB005D
52 0007                      Encrypted Data Key 2, Key Provider ID Length (7)
53 6177732D 6B6D73          Encrypted Data Key 2, Key Provider ID ("aws-kms")
54 004E                      Encrypted Data Key 2, Key Provider Information Length
      (78)
55 61726E3A 6177733A 6B6D733A 63612D63   Encrypted Data Key 2, Key Provider Information ("arn:
      aws:kms:ca-central-1:111122223333:key/9b13ca4b-afcc-46a8-aa47-be3435b423ff")
56 656E7472 616C2D31 3A313131 31323232
57 32333333 333A6B65 792F3962 31336361
58 34622D61 6663632D 34366138 2D616134
59 372D6265 33343335 62343233 6666
60 00A7                      Encrypted Data Key 2, Encrypted Data Key Length (167)
61 01010200 78FAFFFB D6DE06AF AC72F79B   Encrypted Data Key 2, Encrypted Data Key
62 0E57BD87 3F60F4E6 FD196144 5A002C94
63 AF787150 69000000 7E307C06 092A8648
64 86F70D01 0706A06F 306D0201 00306806
65 092A8648 86F70D01 0701301E 06096086
66 48016503 04012E30 11040CB2 A820D0CC
67 76616EF2 A6B30D02 0110803B 8073D0F1
68 FDD01BD9 B0979082 099FDBFC F7B13548
69 3CC686D7 F3CF7C7A CCC52639 122A1495
70 71F18A46 80E2C43F A34C0E58 11D05114
71 2A363C2A E11397
72 01                        Content Type (1, non-framed data)
73 00000000                  Reserved
74 0C                        IV Length (12)
75 00000000                  Frame Length (0, non-framed data)
76 734C1BBE 032F7025 84CDA9D0   IV
77 2C82BB23 4CBF4AAB 8F5C6002 622E886C   Authentication Tag
78 +------+
79 | Body |
80 +------+
81 D39DD3E5 915E0201 77A4AB11   IV
82 00000000 0000028E          Encrypted Content Length (654)
```

```
 83  E8B6F955  B5F22FE4  FD890224  4E1D5155        Encrypted Content
 84  5871BA4C  93F78436  1085E4F8  D61ECE28
 85  59455BD8  D76479DF  C28D2E0B  BDB3D5D3
 86  E4159DFE  C8A944B6  685643FC  EA24122B
 87  6766ECD5  E3F54653  DF205D30  0081D2D8
 88  55FCDA5B  9F5318BC  F4265B06  2FE7C741
 89  C7D75BCC  10F05EA5  0E2F2F40  47A60344
 90  ECE10AA7  559AF633  9DE2C21B  12AC8087
 91  95FE9C58  C65329D1  377C4CD7  EA103EC1
 92  31E4F48A  9B1CC047  EE5A0719  704211E5
 93  B48A2068  8060DF60  B492A737  21B0DB21
 94  C9B21A10  371E6179  78FAFB0B  BAAEC3F4
 95  9D86E334  701E1442  EA5DA288  64485077
 96  54C0C231  AD43571A  B9071925  609A4E59
 97  B8178484  7EB73A4F  AAE46B26  F5B374B8
 98  12B0000C  8429F504  936B2492  AAF47E94
 99  A5BA804F  7F190927  5D2DF651  B59D4C2F
100  A15D0551  DAEBA4AF  2060D0D5  CB1DA4E6
101  5E2034DB  4D19E7CD  EEA6CF7E  549C86AC
102  46B2C979  AB84EE12  202FD6DF  E7E3C09F
103  C2394012  AF20A97E  369BCBDA  62459D3E
104  C6FFB914  FEFD4DE5  88F5AFE1  98488557
105  1BABBAE4  BE55325E  4FB7E602  C1C04BEE
106  F3CB6B86  71666C06  6BF74E1B  0F881F31
107  B731839B  CF711F6A  84CA95F5  958D3B44
108  E3862DF6  338E02B5  C345CFF8  A31D54F3
109  6920AA76  0BF8E903  552C5A04  917CCD11
110  D4E5DF5C  491EE86B  20C33FE1  5D21F0AD
111  6932E67C  C64B3A26  B8988B25  CFA33E2B
112  63490741  3AB79D60  D8AEFBE9  2F48E25A
113  978A019C  FE49EE0A  0E96BF0D  D6074DDB
114  66DFF333  0E10226F  0A1B219C  BE54E4C2
115  2C15100C  6A2AA3F1  88251874  FDC94F6B
116  9247EF61  3E7B7E0D  29F3AD89  FA14A29C
117  76E08E9B  9ADCDF8C  C886D4FD  A69F6CB4
118  E24FDE26  3044C856  BF08F051  1ADAD329
119  C4A46A1E  B5AB72FE  096041F1  F3F3571B
120  2EAFD9CB  B9EB8B83  AE05885A  8F2D2793
121  1E3305D9  0C9E2294  E8AD7E3B  8E4DEC96
122  6276C5F1  A3B7E51E  422D365D  E4C0259C
123  50715406  822D1682  80B0F2E5  5C94
124  65B2E942  24BEEA6E  A513F918  CCEC1DE3        Authentication Tag
125  +--------+
126  | Footer |
127  +--------+
128  0067                                          Signature Length (103)
129  30650230  7229DDF5  B86A5B64  54E4D627        Signature
130  CBE194F1  1CC0F8CF  D27B7F8B  F50658C0
131  BE84B355  3CED1721  A0BE2A1B  8E3F449E
132  1BEB8281  023100B2  0CB323EF  58A4ACE3
133  1559963B  889F72C3  B15D1700  5FB26E61
134  331F3614  BC407CEE  B86A66FA  CBF74D9E
135  34CB7E4B  363A38
```

Framed Data

The following example shows the message format for framed data.

```
 1 +--------+
 2 | Header |
 3 +--------+
 4 01                                      Version (1.0)
 5 80                                      Type (128, customer authenticated encrypted data)
 6 0378                                    Algorithm ID (see [Algorithms Reference](algorithms-
       reference.md))
 7 6E7C0FBD 4DF4A999 717C22A2 DDFE1A27     Message ID (random 128-bit value)
 8 008E                                    AAD Length (142)
 9 0004                                    AAD Key-Value Pair Count (4)
10 0005                                    AAD Key-Value Pair 1, Key Length (5)
11 30746869 73                             AAD Key-Value Pair 1, Key ("0This")
12 0002                                    AAD Key-Value Pair 1, Value Length (2)
13 6973                                    AAD Key-Value Pair 1, Value ("is")
14 0003                                    AAD Key-Value Pair 2, Key Length (3)
15 31616E                                  AAD Key-Value Pair 2, Key ("1an")
16 000A                                    AAD Key-Value Pair 2, Value Length (10)
17 656E6372 79774690 6F6E                  AAD Key-Value Pair 2, Value ("encryption")
18 0008                                    AAD Key-Value Pair 3, Key Length (8)
19 32636F6E 74657874                       AAD Key-Value Pair 3, Key ("2context")
20 0007                                    AAD Key-Value Pair 3, Value Length (7)
21 6578616D 706C65                         AAD Key-Value Pair 3, Value ("example")
22 0015                                    AAD Key-Value Pair 4, Key Length (21)
23 6177732D 63727970 746F2D70 75626C69     AAD Key-Value Pair 4, Key ("aws-crypto-public-key")
24 632D6B65 79
25 0044                                    AAD Key-Value Pair 4, Value Length (68)
26 416A4173 7569326F 7430364C 4B77715A     AAD Key-Value Pair 4, Value ("AjAsui2ot06LKwqZXDJnU/
       Aqc2vD+00kpOZ1cc8Tg2qd7rs5aLTg7lvfUEW/86+/5w==")
27 58444A6E 552F4171 63327644 2B304F6B
28 704F5A31 63633854 67327164 37727335
29 614C5467 376C7666 5545572F 38362B2F
30 35773D3D
31 0002                                    EncryptedDataKeyCount (2)
32 0007                                    Encrypted Data Key 1, Key Provider ID Length (7)
33 6177732D 6B6D73                         Encrypted Data Key 1, Key Provider ID ("aws-kms")
34 004B                                    Encrypted Data Key 1, Key Provider Information Length
       (75)
35 61726E3A 6177733A 6B6D733A 75732D77     Encrypted Data Key 1, Key Provider Information ("arn:
       aws:kms:us-west-2:111122223333:key/715c0818-5825-4245-a755-138a6d9a11e6")
36 6573742D 323A3131 31313232 32323333
37 33333A6B 65792F37 31356330 3831382D
38 35383235 2D343234 352D6137 35352D31
39 33386136 64396131 316536
40 00A7                                    Encrypted Data Key 1, Encrypted Data Key Length (167)
41 01010200 7857A1C1 F7370545 4ECA7C83     Encrypted Data Key 1, Encrypted Data Key
42 956C4702 23DCE8D7 16C59679 973E3CED
43 02A4EF29 7F000000 7E307C06 092A8648
44 86F70D01 0706A06F 306D0201 00306806
45 092A8648 86F70D01 0701301E 06096086
46 48016503 04012E30 11040C3F F02C897B
47 7A12EB19 8BF2D802 0110803B 24003D1F
```

```
48 A5474FBC 392360B5 CB9997E0 6A17DE4C
49 A6BD7332 6BF86DAB 60D8CCB8 8295DBE9
50 4707E356 ADA3735A 7C52D778 B3135A47
51 9F224BF9 E67E87
52 0007                                  Encrypted Data Key 2, Key Provider ID Length (7)
53 6177732D 6B6D73                        Encrypted Data Key 2, Key Provider ID ("aws-kms")
54 004E                                   Encrypted Data Key 2, Key Provider Information Length
     (78)
55 61726E3A 6177733A 6B6D733A 63612D63    Encrypted Data Key 2, Key Provider Information ("arn:
     aws:kms:ca-central-1:111122223333:key/9b13ca4b-afcc-46a8-aa47-be3435b423ff")
56 656E7472 616C2D31 3A313131 31323232
57 32333333 333A6B65 792F3962 31336361
58 34622D61 6663632D 34366138 2D616134
59 372D6265 33343335 62343233 6666
60 00A7                                   Encrypted Data Key 2, Encrypted Data Key Length (167)
61 01010200 78FAFFFB D6DE06AF AC72F79B    Encrypted Data Key 2, Encrypted Data Key
62 0E57BD87 3F60F4E6 FD196144 5A002C94
63 AF787150 69000000 7E307C06 092A8648
64 86F70D01 0706A06F 306D0201 00306806
65 092A8648 86F70D01 0701301E 06096086
66 48016503 04012E30 11040C36 CD985E12
67 D218B674 5BBC6102 0110803B 0320E3CD
68 E470AA27 DEAB660B 3E0CE8E0 8B1A89E4
69 57DCC69B AAB1294F 21202C01 9A50D323
70 72EBAAFD E24E3ED8 7168E0FA DB40508F
71 556FBD58 9E621C
72 02                                     Content Type (2, framed data)
73 00000000                               Reserved
74 0C                                     IV Length (12)
75 00000100                               Frame Length (256)
76 4ECBD5C0 9899CA65 923D2347             IV
77 0B896144 0CA27950 CA571201 4DA58029    Authentication Tag
78 +------+
79 | Body |
80 +------+
81 00000001                               Frame 1, Sequence Number (1)
82 6BD3FE9C ADBCB213 5B89E8F1             Frame 1, IV
83 1F6471E0 A51AF310 10FA9EF6 F0C76EDF    Frame 1, Encrypted Content
84 F5AFA33C 7D2E8C6C 9C5D5175 A212AF8E
85 FBD9A0C3 C6E3FB59 C125DBF2 89AC7939
86 BDEE43A8 0F00F49E ACBBD8B2 1C785089
87 A90DB923 699A1495 C3B31B50 0A48A830
88 201E3AD9 1EA6DA14 7F6496DB 6BC104A4
89 DEB7F372 375ECB28 9BF84B6D 2863889F
90 CB80A167 9C361C4B 5EC07438 7A4822B4
91 A7D9D2CC 5150D414 AF75F509 FCE118BD
92 6D1E798B AEBA4CDB AD009E5F 1A571B77
93 0041BC78 3E5F2F41 8AF157FD 461E959A
94 BB732F27 D83DC36D CC9EBC05 00D87803
95 57F2BB80 066971C2 DEEA062F 4F36255D
96 E866C042 E1382369 12E9926B BA40E2FC
97 A820055F FB47E428 41876F14 3B6261D9
98 5262DB34 59F5D37E 76E46522 E8213640
99 04EE3CC5 379732B5 F56751FA 8E5F26AD    Frame 1, Authentication Tag
```

```
100  00000002                              Frame 2, Sequence Number (2)
101  F1140984 FF25F943 959BE514            Frame 2, IV
102  216C7C6A 2234F395 F0D2D9B9 304670BF   Frame 2, Encrypted Content
103  A1042608 8A8BCB3F B58CF384 D72EC004
104  A41455B4 9A78BAC9 36E54E68 2709B7BD
105  A884C1E1 705FF696 E540D297 446A8285
106  23DFEE28 E74B225A 732F2C0C 27C6BDA2
107  7597C901 65EF3502 546575D4 6D5EBF22
108  1FF787AB 2E38FD77 125D129C 43D44B96
109  778D7CEE 3C36625F FF3A985C 76F7D320
110  ED70B1F3 79729B47 E7D9B5FC 02FCE9F5
111  C8760D55 7779520A 81D54F9B EC45219D
112  95941F7E 5CBAEAC8 CEC13B62 1464757D
113  AC65B6EF 08262D74 44670624 A3657F7F
114  2A57F1FD E7060503 AC37E197 2F297A84
115  DF1172C2 FA63CF54 E6E2B9B6 A86F582B
116  3B16F868 1BBC5E4D 0B6919B3 08D5ABCF
117  FECDC4A4 8577F08B 99D766A1 E5545670
118  A61F0A3B A3E45A84 4D151493 63ECA38F   Frame 2, Authentication Tag
119  FFFFFFFF                              Final Frame, Sequence Number End
120  00000003                              Final Frame, Sequence Number (3)
121  35F74F11 25410F01 DD9E04BF            Final Frame, IV
122  0000008E                              Final Frame, Encrypted Content Length (142)
123  F7A53D37 2F467237 6FBD0B57 D1DFE830   Final Frame, Encrypted Content
124  B965AD1F A910AA5F 5EFFFFF4 BC7D431C
125  BA9FA7C4 B25AF82E 64A04E3A A0915526
126  88859500 7096FABB 3ACAD32A 75CFED0C
127  4A4E52A3 8E41484D 270B7A0F ED61810C
128  3A043180 DF25E5C5 3676E449 0986557F
129  C051AD55 A437F6BC 139E9E55 6199FD60
130  6ADC017D BA41CDA4 C9F17A83 3823F9EC
131  B66B6A5A 80FDB433 8A48D6A4 21CB
132  811234FD 8D589683 51F6F39A 040B3E3B   Final Frame, Authentication Tag
133  +--------+
134  | Footer |
135  +--------+
136  0066                                  Signature Length (102)
137  30640230 085C1D3C 63424E15 B2244448   Signature
138  639AED00 F7624854 F8CF2203 D7198A28
139  758B309F 5EFD9D5D 2E07AD0B 467B8317
140  5208B133 02301DF7 2DFC877A 66838028
141  3C6A7D5E 4F8B894E 83D98E7C E350F424
142  7E06808D 0FE79002 E24422B9 98A0D130
143  A13762FF 844D
```

109

AWS Encryption SDK Algorithms Reference

> The information on this page is a reference for building your own encryption library that is compatible with the AWS Encryption SDK. If you are not building your own compatible encryption library, you likely do not need this information. To use the AWS Encryption SDK in one of the supported programming languages, see Programming Languages.

To build your own library that can read and write ciphertexts that are compatible with the AWS Encryption SDK, you should understand how the SDK implements the supported algorithms to encrypt raw data. The SDK supports nine algorithm suites. An implementation specifies the encryption algorithm and mode, encryption key length, key derivation algorithm (if one applies), and signature algorithm (if one applies). The following table contains an overview of each implementation. By default, the SDK uses the first implementation in the following table. The list that follows the table provides more information.

AWS Encryption SDK Algorithm Suites

Algorithm ID (in 2-byte hex)	Algorithm Name	Data Key Length (in bits)	Algorithm Mode	IV Length (in bytes)	Authentication Tag Length (in bytes)	Key Derivation Algorithm	Signature Algorithm
03 78	AES	256	GCM	12	16	HKDF with SHA-384	ECDSA with P-384 and SHA-384
03 46	AES	192	GCM	12	16	HKDF with SHA-384	ECDSA with P-384 and SHA-384
02 14	AES	128	GCM	12	16	HKDF with SHA-256	ECDSA with P-256 and SHA-256
01 78	AES	256	GCM	12	16	HKDF with SHA-256	Not applicable
01 46	AES	192	GCM	12	16	HKDF with SHA-256	Not applicable
01 14	AES	128	GCM	12	16	HKDF with SHA-256	Not applicable
00 78	AES	256	GCM	12	16	Not applicable	Not applicable
00 46	AES	192	GCM	12	16	Not applicable	Not applicable
00 14	AES	128	GCM	12	16	Not applicable	Not applicable

Algorithm ID

A 2-byte value that uniquely identifies an algorithm's implementation. This value is stored in the ciphertext's message header.

110

Algorithm Name

The encryption algorithm used. For all algorithm suites, the SDK uses the Advanced Encryption Standard (AES) encryption algorithm.

Data Key Length

The length of the data key. The SDK supports 256-bit, 192-bit, and 128-bit keys. The data key is generated by a master key. For some implementations, this data key is used as input to an HMAC-based extract-and-expand key derivation function (HKDF). The output of the HKDF is used as the data encryption key in the encryption algorithm. For more information, see **Key Derivation Algorithm** in this list.

Algorithm Mode

The mode used with the encryption algorithm. For all algorithm suites, the SDK uses Galois/Counter Mode (GCM).

IV Length

The length of the initialization vector (IV) used with AES-GCM.

Authentication Tag Length

The length of the authentication tag used with AES-GCM.

Key Derivation Algorithm

The HMAC-based extract-and-expand key derivation function (HKDF) used to derive the data encryption key. The SDK uses the HKDF defined in RFC 5869, with the following specifics:

- The hash function used is either SHA-384 or SHA-256, as specified by the algorithm ID.
- For the extract step:
  - No salt is used. Per the RFC, this means that the salt is set to a string of zeros. The string length is equal to the length of the hash function output; that is, 48 bytes for SHA-384 and 32 bytes for SHA-256.
  - The input keying material is the data key received from the master key provider.
- For the expand step:
  - The input pseudorandom key is the output from the extract step.
  - The input info is a concatenation of the algorithm ID followed by the message ID.
  - The length of the output keying material is the **Data Key Length** described previously. This output is used as the data encryption key in the encryption algorithm.

Signature Algorithm

The signature algorithm used to generate a signature over the ciphertext header and body. The SDK uses the Elliptic Curve Digital Signature Algorithm (ECDSA) with the following specifics:

- The elliptic curve used is either the P-384 or P-256 curve, as specified by the algorithm ID. These curves are defined in Digital Signature Standard (DSS) (FIPS PUB 186-4).
- The hash function used is SHA-384 (with the P-384 curve) or SHA-256 (with the P-256 curve).

AWS Encryption SDK Initialization Vector Reference

The information on this page is a reference for building your own encryption library that is compatible with the AWS Encryption SDK. If you are not building your own compatible encryption library, you likely do not need this information. To use the AWS Encryption SDK in one of the supported programming languages, see Programming Languages.

The AWS Encryption SDK supplies the initialization vectors (IVs) that are required by all supported algorithm suites. The SDK uses frame sequence numbers to construct an IV so that no two frames in the same message can have the same IV.

Each IV is constructed from two big-endian byte arrays concatenated in the following order:

- 64 bytes: 0 (reserved for future use)
- 32 bytes: Frame sequence number. For the header authentication tag, this value is all zeroes.

Before the introduction of data key caching, the AWS Encryption SDK always used a new data key to encrypt each message, and it generated all IVs randomly. Randomly generated IVs were cryptographically safe because data keys were never reused. When the SDK introduced data key caching, which intentionally reuses data keys, we changed the way the SDK generates IVs.

Using deterministic IVs that cannot repeat within a message significantly increases the number of invocations that can safely be executed under a single data key. In addition, data keys that are cached always use an algorithm suite with a key derivation function. Using a deterministic IV with a pseudo-random key derivation function to derive encryption keys from a data key allows the AWS Encryption SDK to encrypt 2^{32} messages without exceeding cryptographic bounds.

Document History for the AWS Encryption SDK Developer Guide

The following table describes the significant changes to this documentation.

Latest documentation update: March 21, 2017

Change	Description	Date
New release	Added the Data Key Caching chapter for the new feature. Added the AWS Encryption SDK Initialization Vector Reference topic that explains that the SDK changed from generating random IVs to constructing deterministic IVs. Added the Concepts in the AWS Encryption SDK topic to explain concepts, including the new cryptographic materials manager.	July 31, 2017
Update	Expanded the Message Format Reference documentation into a new AWS Encryption SDK Reference section. Added a section about the AWS Encryption SDK's Supported Algorithm Suites.	March 21, 2017
New release	The AWS Encryption SDK now supports the Python programming language, in addition to Java.	March 21, 2017
Initial release	Initial release of the AWS Encryption SDK and this documentation.	March 22, 2016

www.ingramcontent.com/pod-product-compliance
Lightning Source LLC
LaVergne TN
LVHW082040050326
832904LV00005B/248